Lincoln and Douglas

Jan Jacobi

Reedy Press
PO Box 5131
St. Louis, MO 63139, USA
reedypress.com

Library of Congress Control Number: 2024948779

ISBN: 9781681065816

Cover Illustration: David Zamudio
Line Art: Adapted from clip art courtesy of Getty, Alamy, Freepik, and in the public domain.

Printed in the United States of America
25 26 27 28 29 5 4 3 2 1

Dedication

For Robert Bray and Michael Burlingame

Scholars, Teachers, Mentors, and Friends

Table of Contents

Preface

"My friends—No one, not in my situation, can appreciate my feeling of sadness at this parting. To this place, and the kindness of these people, I owe every thing. Here I have lived a quarter of a century, and have passed from a young to an old man. Here my children have been born, and one is buried. I now leave, not knowing when, or whether ever, I may return, with a task before me greater than that which rested upon Washington. Without the assistance of that Divine Being, who ever attended him, I cannot succeed. With that assistance I cannot fail. Trusting in Him, who can go with me, and remain with you and be every where for good, let us confidently hope that all will yet be well. To His care commending you, as I hope in your prayers you will commend me, I bid you an affectionate farewell."

Lincoln's Farewell Address
Springfield, Illinois
February 12, 1861

PART ONE

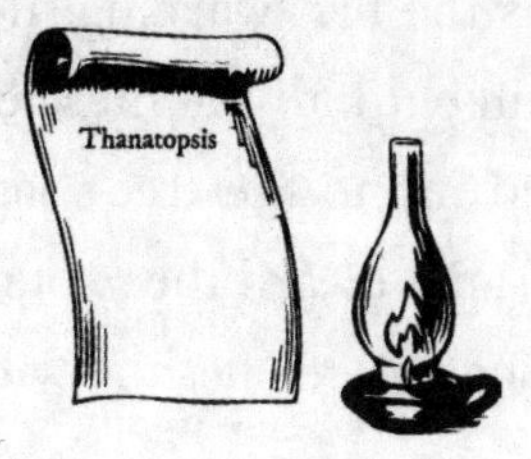

Chapter 1

This Was a Sad Trip

The sound was the first warning. It was a loud crack. A searing pain cut into the muscles of my back. The rope, which bound me to the tree's jagged bark, slipped slightly. My head sank toward the ground. The next crack felt like a nail ripping into my flesh. Trying to steady myself, I gritted my teeth.

The cracks came like gunshots. One after the other they turned my back into red pulp. I could see bits of my flesh clinging to the brown stalks of the dying grass. As I sagged down the tree's trunk, the bark cut into my chest. My blood spilled onto the dry ground. Worst were the jolting spasms of pain when the lashes struck the open wounds.

Why were they trying to kill me? What had I done?

I could bear it no longer. I felt myself slipping away and tumbling into the darkness.

I awoke to a procession of phantom shapes: black shadows and white ghosts that swept past me into the vapor. The ghoulish apparitions continued to march toward an abyss. Gradually the shapes became human, and I saw, hovering together in grief, my mother and father, and my wife and children. I had no feeling for them. They became a multitude of black forms swirling chaotically toward a roiling sea. The waves broke over them and carried them out into deeper water. "Avenge us!" was their drowning cry. Then came white forms dancing across a field. That moment of mirth turned to terror when a violent explosion shook the earth. From the nearby woods a flash fire rushed out onto the field and devoured them. In the rubble of the scorched countryside was something that looked like a charred rock, but from its underside emerged tiny, webbed membranes that formed primitive legs and feet. A serpentine head poked out tentatively. It appeared to be the only survivor.

My head cleared, and I was on a steamboat. On my wrist was an iron manacle from which a short chain tied me to a longer, heavier one. Five other men were bound to the stronger chain in a similar manner. We looked like so many fish upon a trot line.

We had no idea how long the voyage would last. We ate, languished, and slept together in our chains. When we wet and soiled ourselves, we had to live in our own waste. The ship's hold, where we were kept, reeked of waste and rot. I sickened and vomited up my food.

Where were we going? If we survived this ordeal, would a worse one await us?

When the ship docked, we were thrown into carts for transport to another unknown location.

It was a house in the middle of the city. No one lived there.

On the first day, the owner, a well-dressed gentleman, led me into an elegant room. He ordered me to take off my clothes. I refused. He whistled and a rough man with a whip appeared. The owner told me if I didn't comply, his assistant would beat me mercilessly until I did.

The rough man stripped me of my clothes. I was standing naked before them.

The owner examined me from the front and from the back. I felt his hand testing the muscles in my shoulders, my arms, my thighs, and my legs. He pried open my mouth and inspected the teeth in my upper and lower jaws.

"A fine specimen, what a fine specimen," he said to himself. "When his back heals, this one will get well over one thousand."

"Where am I going?" I asked him.

"To hell for all I care," he said coldly. . . .

"Husband, husband," came Molly's frightened cry, "what has happened?"

I was shaking violently.

"You were calling for help, and I decided to wake you."

For a moment, I was still in the land between my frightful dream and the inside of our carriage.

"I dozed off. It was a dreadful dream. I thought I was a slave from Kentucky who ran off but was captured and beaten. My owner decided to sell me into the deep South and shipped me to New Orleans. In the auction house, I was stripped and threatened with another beating—and then you woke me."

"Mr. Lincoln, you are agitated by slavery."

"My dear, my dreams have sometimes been meaningless, though sometimes they are portents. I fear this one may be portentous."

"Do not worry. Clay and Douglas will settle it. I have faith in them."

Though I flinched at the name of Douglas, I granted her the point.

She pushed back in her seat, balanced her head on the cushion behind her, and closed her eyes. Now it was Molly's turn to rest.

I looked out the window.

The carriage road from Louisville to Lexington was covered with brown, dried leaves. Only a few weeks earlier, they had decked the countryside with shades of red, orange, and yellow. Now the trees were yielding the rest of their dead leaves to the insistent winds of early winter. The blue green of the Kentucky grass was fading to a lighter brown, and the goldenrod stalks bowed over and released their fluffy seeds into the wind.

The cold air seeped into the comfortable passenger cabin of the coach in which we were riding to visit Molly's family. As I placed my arm around her, I could see that the tension and sadness of the past months were still hanging on her face. On July 17, 1849, her father, Robert S. Todd, had died of cholera, a victim of the disease that swept across the country in the summer.

Distance kept us from attending his funeral, and we had not seen Molly's family since his death. It was already October 29, and we had timed the visit for me to join Mr. Todd's lawyer in settling his estate.

I glanced at Molly and then looked out the window again. Much of our passage was over the rolling hills of north central Kentucky. The subdued hues of the countryside signaled the transition to grayer days and colder nights. As we approached Lexington, the terrain eased into level fields.

Should I waken Molly? No, I thought—let her sleep and get some solace before the difficult arrival at the Todd family house.

For Molly, the death of her father opened wounds that never fully healed. Rich, cultivated, and sure of himself, Robert Todd married Eliza Parker, the daughter of another prominent Lexington family. Tragically, Eliza died of fever after giving birth to her seventh child.

The loss of her mother devastated Molly. Equally disheartening, within months of her mother's death, her father began a relationship with a younger woman. A year and a half later they were married. Over the years, Molly and her siblings were joined by another eight half-brothers and sisters.

Her father was rarely home. When the family moved to a larger house on Main Street, Molly's stepmother was overwhelmed. The children were raised by the family slaves. The love and affection of Mammy Sally and Grandmother Parker saved Molly.

We turned onto a cobblestone road that took us into central Lexington and her childhood home. The uneven surface jolted Molly awake.

"What has happened?" she cried.

"We have arrived in Lexington."

She shielded her face from the afternoon sun and looked up at me.

"Why didn't you wake me before?" she asked.

"You were fast asleep. I thought it would keep you from worry. You've not slept well these past months."

She did not reply, and I looked out at the large white houses and their spacious grounds.

"You have been very kind to me since he died," she said softly.

"You have been so unhappy. There was no warning," I counseled, and then added, "but thank goodness Grandmother Parker is alive."

"When I was very young, her house was next door. She took me under her wing when my mother died. She was so devoted to all of us."

"And to you in particular?"

"Yes, when Mother died, she was distraught for weeks, but reaching out to me helped her live with it."

"Why you and not one of the others?"

"I don't really know. My earliest memories are of being with Grandmother Parker. I sensed I was special to her. She loved to read to us, and I was the one who always stayed and asked for another story. She took me to the dressmaker's shop more often than the others, and she gave me a pony when I was six. It was just before Mother died."

"We'll see her tonight or tomorrow morning."

"Oh, I do hope it is tonight, and I can't wait to see my sweet sister Emilie."

The carriage drew up to a large brick house on Main Street. This was the house to which Robert Todd had moved his family in 1832.

Standing on the front steps and on the sidewalk surrounding the house was a bevy of Todd relations—Molly's stepmother cloaked in black, her brothers and half-brothers in dark suits and sisters and half-sisters in long dresses, older children subdued in their manner and dress, and a host of small fry wiggling through the legs of their elders.

Molly emerged through the door and down the carriage steps, and I followed. The crowd of welcomers parted so Molly could greet her stepmother, Betsey.

"I'm so glad you have come," Betsey said warmly, "and I hope your journey wasn't too strenuous."

Molly hugged her tightly and gave her a kiss on the cheek.

Once this formality was over, the welcomers poured forward in a wave that broke over us with joy and sadness.

The inside of the house was luxurious. There were fourteen rooms. Downstairs were double parlors for formal occasions, such as a visit from Henry Clay, and a parlor for the more relaxed family gatherings. The dining room featured a large oval mahogany table that had come from England. Mr. Todd's extensive library was displayed in bookshelves throughout the house. Adjacent to the dining room was the pantry where the slaves gathered to serve the meals. Upstairs were the bedrooms.

Molly's sister Emilie escorted us to one of the guest bedrooms and told us that Grandmother Parker, who was not in the welcoming reception, would be coming to supper. We were given the opportunity to freshen ourselves before the evening meal.

At supper, Grandmother Parker was seated at the foot of the table with Molly and me on either side. Elizabeth Rittenhouse Porter Parker was eighty years old and frail, but her agile mind and animated presence made her seem younger. When she looked at Molly, her eyes sparkled, and she smiled approvingly.

"Mary dear," she said, "tell me about your children. Let's start with that young fellow who is named for your father."

Molly looked briefly at me and then replied, "Bobby has just turned six. He reminds me of Father. I rather think he'll turn out to be a Todd and not a Lincoln. He's lively and mischievous, but then he turns serious and reserved. I think it's because he misses his father who is away so often with the other lawyers trying cases on the circuit."

"Remember, my dear, that your father was often away from home. Young Robert will take after both the Todds and the Lincolns," Grandmother Parker responded, giving me a stealthy smile.

"And the second one?" she asked.

"Our dear Eddie," said Molly quietly, almost as if a cloud had crossed her face. "He is such a kind, sweet boy. He adores us both. He spends most of his time trying to keep up with Bobby."

"We are worried about him," I added. "He has been sickly this last year. He seemed weaker just before we left to come here."

"God bless the dear one. I know you'll take care of him," Grandmother Parker told us.

The following day, in the late morning, I walked to courthouse Square to meet with Mr. Todd's lawyer. His office was on the third floor in a building adjacent to the Courthouse. I found it easily and rapped on the door.

George "Old Buster" Robertson welcomed me warmly. He was a large man with a mop of disheveled, graying-reddish hair; lively hazel eyes; a red, bulbous nose; and a full auburn beard. His protruding belly rolled out over his belt, and his fraying pant cuffs brushed over his well-worn shoes. He was working his jaw strenuously on a quid of tobacco. When he turned to deposit a stream of brown saliva into a wide-mouth pot by his desk, he missed, which accounted for the stains on the floor.

He motioned me to the chair in front of his desk while seating himself behind it. After clearing his throat and spitting once more into the pot, he eyed me and asked, "Good trip?"

"As good as it could be given the circumstances."

"How's the missus?"

"Not well," I admitted.

"It's no surprise," he countered. "Things were never the same after her mother died. He tried to help them adjust to Betsey, but they never cottoned to her. It got a little better when all those brothers and sisters rolled out. What did the old man make of you?"

I hesitated and thought a moment before I replied.

He took this for a demurral and blurted, "Well, what did you make of him?"

"We got on very well. Molly was one of his favorites, and that certainly helped. As you know, he was very good to us."

"And you fancied his friend, old man Clay, didn't you? Birds of a feather in politics? That must have helped."

"We were both Whigs, and we had similar views on the slavery issue."

Old Buster started to cough and splutter. Some of his tobacco juice must have gone down the wrong pipe. As he hacked and wheezed, his face reddened. I rose to slap him on the back, but he waved me off.

Gradually the coughing subsided, and he managed to say haltingly, "Old . . . Harry's . . . back . . . at . . . it. He's trying to get enough of them to stitch together a compromise on that territory we stole from the Mexicans."

I paused and looked toward the window.

Loud voices came from outside, and it sounded like a disturbance. Old Buster didn't notice. The shouting outside became an uproar.

"Is there something going on out there?" I asked.

He looked over at the window and took out his pocket watch.

"Yes, I forgot about it. It's the slave auction. Noon on Thursdays. Go take a look if you want."

I accepted his invitation and walked over to a large window overlooking the square. I pushed it up and leaned out slightly.

Directly under us was the auction block, and standing on it was a frightened young negro woman.

Around her was a frenzied crowd of a hundred or more men. They wore all manner of clothes: some in finery, most in common dress, and a few in shabby coats covering ragged shirts and pants. All were pressing in for a closer look.

I was horrified and alarmed for the young woman.

The auctioneer, a well-dressed man, climbed onto the block and yelled to the crowd.

"Get up here and takc a look at this fine specimen."

No one moved.

After a moment, a man came forward, and the auctioneer helped him up onto the block. He stepped toward the trembling woman and told her to turn around. He placed his hands on her shoulders, stroked her back, and then brushed them over her buttocks. She winced and tried to pull away from him.

"Not so fast, my girl," he countered. The crowd urged him on. He pulled her around, and repeated his advances cupping his hands on her breasts. The leering throng swelled forward expecting him to remove her shirt.

Turning toward the auctioneer, he shouted, "I'll give you two hundred for this lovely creature."

"Sold," yelled the auctioneer as he rapped his hammer on the block.

The young woman collapsed with a piercing shriek followed by primordial wails that echoed around the square. These were succeeded by uncontrollable sobs and moans. No one could fail to be affected by her grief.

"Oh, my sweet Cecilia, you are gone from me forever. My child, they are taking me away."

I could bear it no longer. My dream had foreshadowed this tragedy; the reality was even worse.

After closing the window, I leaned forward and held onto the sill with my large hands. I stared down at the blue veins running underneath the surface of my white skin. What gave us the right to be so cruel to our fellow creatures? I continued my meditation for a minute or two.

Old Buster must have noticed.

"What was it?" he asked. "Another darky mother mourning the loss of her child?"

"Yes," I said flatly.

"You'd get used to it if you lived down here."

"I hope not," I replied.

"You would, Lincoln," he said. "They don't have the same feelings we do. They're the same as the horses, the cows, and the hogs. Even a sow squeals when one of her little oinkers is taken from her. Tomorrow morning when she's on her way to whatever godforsaken place she's going, she'll have forgotten it. Only thing on her mind will be pleasing her new mas'r."

I was deeply disturbed by what I had seen and what he had said.

"I might like to take a walk," I said. "I need a little time to think."

"Take a walk? Think?" he upbraided me. "And what do you think you'll see on your walk? See that poplar tree next to the auction block? See those three mighty limbs coming out from the stump? Well, if you wait until the auction's done, you'll have a chance to see this afternoon's whippings. Big white overseer can't wait for it. Brute of a man. Ties one of 'em black devils to the tree and whips him till he's almost gone. Lash by lash until his back is mashed into a gushing flow of red."

"What has anyone done to deserve that?"

"Probably slinking around after dark."

He continued, "And then walk another block over toward Eliza Parker's house, and you'll stumble onto Robards's slave pen. Crams 'em in there. Pays low for the sickly ones, fattens 'em up, and sells high. Right across is the place where Robards keeps the mulatto girls. Gussies 'em up and then strips 'em for the tom cats who are on the prowl. They fetch a hefty price.

"It's a business, Lincoln. It's our way of life."

"Do you own slaves, Robertson?"

"I do."

"What I don't understand is how you can own them when you know they are being cruelly mistreated."

Old Buster looked at me as if I were a naive schoolboy. His face softened, and he adopted the manner of a patient schoolteacher trying to make his point to a country simpleton.

"We don't mistreat them. Why would we do that? They cook our food and serve it to us at our dining room tables, they clean our houses and wash our clothes, and they raise our children. Many of us loved our mammies more than our own mothers. Do you see them mistreated at the Todd House?"

"Surely you can't justify the entire system based on a few exceptions."

Old Buster supposed he was the cat who caught the mouse.

"Lincoln, your reasoning is flawed. The exception is the slaveowner who is cruel."

Old Buster spat into his pot once more. He cut himself another piece from his plug and settled it into the natural pouch of his left cheek. He rose from his chair, pulled up his pants, and marched to the center of the office.

"Lincoln, you don't seem yourself," he observed. "Why don't you come back tomorrow and we can finish up the estate."

On the short walk home, I was troubled by what I had witnessed an hour earlier. While I had watched slave auctions with repugnance in New Orleans when I was a young man, and while they left a lasting impression, I had to admit they did not affect me as perhaps they should have. At Speed's plantation and at the Todd home, I was served by slaves—by slaves attending to me alone—and while I felt uncomfortable, the feeling receded as a dream does when we first emerge from sleep.

Should I have represented Matson in his suit against the abolitionists who harbored his runaway slaves? My first inclination had been to take the side of the runaways, but why didn't I honor it? I still remembered the time on the steamboat from Louisville to St. Louis when Speed and I looked down from the deck onto the chained slaves.

Sometimes it came to me in a dream and jarred me awake. Why had I misjudged the slaves' feelings? How could I have possibly believed they were happy? These questions haunted me as I walked back to the Todd house.

When I reached it, I entered through the front door and walked into the family parlor. There I found Molly, her sister Emilie, and Grandmother Parker drinking coffee and enjoying a lively conversation.

Molly looked up at me and said, "My dear Emilie has just been saying she'd like to visit us in Springfield next year."

"She'd be more than welcomed," I said, smiling at Emilie.

She blushed and responded, "I could also visit Elizabeth, Frances, and Anne."

"A lovely idea, my sweet," cooed Molly.

They turned to each other and began to chat about all the things Emilie could do in Springfield. While it couldn't compete with Lexington, there were traveling entertainments that enlivened Springfield's cultural and social life.

I was sitting next to Grandmother Parker. She was as lively as ever, but as I looked more closely at her face, I noticed that she looked tired and a bit pale. Her eyes had lost their sparkle.

"Grandmother Parker," I said, "I have a question for you."

"Please, you must ask me whatever you wish."

"What are your views on slavery?"

"Oh, Mr. Lincoln, I have listened to so many men speak their piece on slavery that I wondered whether any of them cared what a woman thought. Robert and Harry Clay wanted to return them to Africa. I never liked that. Those who wish to go should have the choice, but they should not be forced to return. For better or for worse, their lives have become entwined with ours."

"What does that mean? Are you in favor of abolition?"

"No, but I do believe in gradual emancipation. You do know that when I die, my slaves will be freed."

I was stunned. "Does the family know?"

"Mr. Robertson has told the family, and I spoke to Mary this morning."

"That is courageous, Grandmother Parker."

"I am glad you approve."

I was still trying to gather myself. This was so unexpected that I couldn't quite comprehend it. For one of Lexington's leading citizens and for the elder of the Todd and Parker families to free her slaves was a fateful choice.

"Some of my slaves have been with me for sixty years. They have been my family. I cannot imagine them sold to someone else—their families torn apart and some in the hands of heartless, brutal masters. I do not know about national policy. I will leave that to Harry Clay. I do know about family, and I want them to be free.

"I have provided for their shelter and their education," she continued. "Some may stay in Kentucky, and others may go north where free negroes are more welcomed."

"I wish we were more welcoming in Illinois," I said.

On the night before we were to return to Springfield, after dinner we had a final family gathering in the formal parlor. One by one, they retired for the evening, but I lingered.

Perhaps I wished to take in the ornate setting once more—the embroidered draperies, the Turkish carpeting, and the exquisite furniture—or perhaps I wished to ponder my thoughts from the past few days.

They all drifted back to slavery.

The crusty realism of Old Buster, contrasted with Grandmother Parker's beneficent decision to free her slaves. Where was I on this issue that threatened to pull our country apart?

I had always felt slavery to be an injustice, but when I was in Congress, Joshua Giddings tried to persuade me it was a moral issue. The next logical step was abolition. Giddings was the leading abolitionist in the Whig Party.

I believed abolition would lead to civil war. I could not take that step. There would have to be a compromise which could satisfy the southern states and keep them in the Union. I resolved to wait and see if Henry Clay could work his magic once more.

I stood up and walked over to the bookshelves. Paging through one of these books, I stumbled onto a poem by William Cullen Bryant titled "Thanatopsis." It was a meditation on death. I memorized it and then lingered on one line: ". . . Make thee to shudder, and grow sick at heart . . ."

I wondered whether Robert Smith Todd had "shuddered and grown sick at heart."

He had not expected to die. He was in good health. Henry and Lucretia Clay survived the same illness. He thought he would recover.

When did he first know he would die? What, if anything, gave him strength in that darkening hour? Was it his religious faith? Did he feel himself being carried out of this world and into another? Those who were with him reported he was calm and peaceful in his last hours. What gave him heart?

The following morning and early afternoon, we readied ourselves for the coach ride to Louisville where we would stay overnight. We were set for a three o'clock departure. Family arrived for breakfast and dinner, and at 2:30, a large group of them assembled by the front steps. They had welcomed us so warmly over the two weeks that it was hard to leave. Particularly poignant was our farewell to Grandmother Parker. Molly spent most of her visit re-connecting with her. They were in tears. When she gave me her blessing, my eyes watered.

Molly was overcome with emotion and said nothing as our coach departed. Gradually she settled into a gentle rest which then became comforting sleep. I looked out the window to see Lexington slipping away. After a while, twilight began to settle over the hills and fields. It was followed by dusk and first darkness. The natural rhythms of the day and night were always a comfort for me.

The carriage lurched when we hit a washed-out spot in the road. Molly awoke and slowly gathered herself.

"How far are we?" she asked.

"Probably about half way. You slept soundly."

"I was so tired. This was a sad trip."

She continued, "There was something from this morning that I didn't tell you. A letter came from Elizabeth. She wrote that Eddie was better for the first few days, but that his fever has returned and worsened. There were spells when he could hardly breathe."

"They've been so uncertain about what it is and what will happen to the poor little fellow," I replied.

At first Eddie's illnesses seemed childhood maladies that came and went. When they passed, he was once again the cheerful, dear boy who loved his parents and his older brother. Wherever Bobby went, there was Eddie trailing after. They were inseparable.

"We will just have to hope for the best," I said.

Molly said nothing, turned toward the window, and peered out into the darkness.

Chapter 2

It Was Wrapped in a Shroud of Darkness

The walk from our house on Eighth and Jackson to the Lincoln and Herndon law office on the town square was four blocks north and three blocks west. If I had an appointment, I walked there directly, but if not, I could meander a block over and a block up. There were often friends to greet, and small conversations with each one. Dogs and children bounced past me, sometimes acknowledging my presence.

The day after we returned from Kentucky, Springfield was covered with a few inches of early winter snow. No one was in the streets as I walked to the office. The wind carried the sweeping white flakes into my face. I hadn't wrapped my muffler carefully, and they buried down into my neck.

I knocked the snow from my boots and climbed the stairs to the third floor of the Tinsley Building and opened our office door, which lacked center and upper panels. Crouched over a small table near the rusty, antique stove, already at work on the day's briefs for pending cases, sat Billy Herndon.

Billy paused from his labors, looked up eagerly, and exclaimed, "Lincoln, I wasn't expecting you this morning."

"My friend," I replied, "I am here and delighted to see you. I am glad to be home."

Billy's cheerful greeting caused me to reflect on our partnership for a moment. I chose Billy to be my partner in the fall of 1844. Two weeks earlier, he was licensed to practice law in Illinois. He had never tried a case.

I was asked why I hired such an inexperienced man to be my partner. "Why, he is the best man for the job," I replied. Ten years younger than I, Billy had grown into a respected lawyer and devoted family man in the fifteen years since I first met him. He had tempered the impulsive behavior of his youth but retained his youthful optimism and some of his political radicalism. On slavery, he was becoming an abolitionist.

Over the years Billy became an invaluable partner. He happily researched our most difficult cases in the law library at the Capitol. When I prepared the briefs, I appreciated the detailed work he had done for me. For a time he managed the office and our books efficiently, but unfortunately he slipped into some of my sloppy habits, and the office started to look as unkempt as my hair.

He also became a friend, and I appreciated his loyalty. While I was in Washington for two years, Billy held the firm together. My faith in him was unquestioned.

"How was your time in Lexington?" he asked.

"Fair to middlin', I'd say. There are too many Todds to keep track of them all."

"How is Mrs. Lincoln?"

I looked around the room, focused briefly on the newspapers on Billy's table, and then said slowly, "Not well, I'm afraid." I paused and then added, "She's distressed that she wasn't with her father before he died. I was hoping she'd find some peace during the visit, but she didn't. It will just take more time."

"How is your little one?"

I could hardly speak, looked down at the floor, and replied, "Not well, either. His coughing is keeping him up most of the night. Molly is constantly with him. Neither of us is sleeping."

I walked over to the window, which was covered with snow, soot, and dirt.

Trying to peer through it, I said, "Billy, this window is so filthy that it's impossible to see anything."

"Lincoln, it may be a metaphor for what's happening in our country."

I eased over to the couch, plopped down, stretched out my long frame, made myself as comfortable as I could, and then cradled my head on one of the threadbare pillows. I knew I was in for a squall.

Billy's routine was to read the daily newspapers before I arrived at the office. He always greeted me with a summary of national events.

Since the end of the Mexican War, slavery had re-emerged as the burning national issue.

Everything was changing. The question facing the country was whether slavery should be allowed to expand into the territories—in the land we'd acquired from Mexico and land from the Louisiana Purchase that had not yet been settled.

For thirty years, the Missouri Compromise, negotiated by Henry Clay, held us together by ensuring an equal number of slave and free states.

"Lincoln, this time it's different. It's much more complicated."

"Slow down, my young friend," I counseled him. "Henry Clay is riding a white horse once more. The Great Compromiser will pull us back from the breach."

Billy became more agitated. Prowling around the office like a caged animal, he spoke faster as his face reddened.

"You aren't listening," he sputtered. "Not even Henry Clay will be able to solve it. There are extremists on both sides that won't vote for his plan. There aren't enough senators in the middle."

"He's a magician, Billy. Old Buster Robertson told me he will get the votes."

He hovered over me. Then, like a wrestler maneuvering to pin me, he finished with a grand flourish.

"Henry Clay will not be able to do it. When the pieces fall apart, there is only one person who will be able to put them together."

"And who is that?"

"Stephen A. Douglas," he replied.

Taking notice of this, I sat up, glared at him, and said, "If that happens, he will be perfectly positioned to run for president in 1852. Imagine that, the Little Giant as president at the age of thirty-eight—the youngest man in the history of the republic to be elected president. It might happen if he can control his drinking."

Billy smiled and said emphatically, "That certainly changes the subject!"

I laughed and asked him, "Do you remember when Richard Young gave a champagne party to celebrate his election to the Senate? At the end of the evening, Douglas and Shields were seen dancing on the tables, smashing dishes and kicking the bottles onto the floor."

As the image came back to us, we could hardly contain our laughter.

Circling back to his previous point, Billy added, "He has earned his success; you can't begrudge him that."

"True," I said.

"He's had more success than any Democrat his age since Jefferson," he added.

"Probably true as well."

"The counterpart to Henry Clay."

I did not reply to this indignity.

"And what about his maiden speech in the House? He defended Andrew Jackson and received a letter of appreciation from the old man himself. In your maiden speech, you attacked Polk and the Mexican War and lost half your constituents."

"Billy, remember the story of the tortoise and the hare."

"Lincoln, if you are in that race, you are half a mile behind the tortoise."

"ENOUGH, William!" I barked at him and then fell back on the couch and stared at the ceiling.

My thoughts turned to Douglas. Everyone in Illinois knew him as Judge Douglas. The title had stuck after his term on the Illinois Supreme Court.

I first met Douglas in Vandalia at the legislative session of 1834–35. The meeting was unremarkable. We did little more than observe that one of us was tall and the other short.

Upon first meeting him, one noted that his physique was deceiving. Perhaps more revealing was the huge size of his head. Framed by his dark brown hair were a prominent forehead, imposing eyebrows, intense deep blue eyes, a well-proportioned nose, and a strong, square jaw. Because his shoulders and trunk were broad, he did not seem diminutive. His shortness was in his legs, just as my height was in mine.

It was his manner that defined him. Energetic and charming, he thrived on the vitality of political life. Always in motion, he was known early as a "steam engine in britches." He was forceful and determined—a whirlwind of energy and ambition. Brilliant and supremely confident, he was combative in politics while working tirelessly for his party. Sometimes blustery, sometimes manipulative, he pursued his objectives relentlessly.

As greenhorn lawyers, we were fortunate to settle in Springfield, the new state capital of Illinois. I lived with Joshua Speed above his store on the town square, and Douglas settled in Jacksonville, a town just west of Springfield. He joined the rising men of Springfield during our convivial evenings by the fireplace in Speed's store. When politics arose, we did our best to keep the discussions civil, but I found that a rip-roaring political argument with Douglas could clarify my thinking and sharpen my skills as a debater.

Since I was a Whig and he was a Democrat, fierce ambition and political rivalry often divided us, but underneath the conflict, there was always an understanding. We respected and liked each other, and we became friends.

Billy lumbered over to the window and stood by it momentarily.

"Is it any clearer now?" I asked.

"Just as murky as ever."

"But, Billy, what is that green sprout by your foot?"

He looked down and laughed.

"Lincoln, do you remember those seeds you took to Washington to give the other congressmen as an offering from the farmers of Illinois? It appears that you brought some of those packages back home, and one of the seeds fell on the floor. The fellow who sweeps our office seems to have piled enough dirt onto it, and the leak from the window must have given it the water it needed to grow.

"So what should we do about it?" he asked.

"Can you bring a pot from somewhere?" I responded.

"I can probably do that."

"Excellent. Then we can plant it in your pot, put it on the window sill, and keep it alive until the spring.

"Did any new cases sprout while I was away?" I asked.

Billy shuffled through the files and found the folder he wanted.

"This is a new one, a slander case in Shelby County Circuit Court. There appears to have been tension between one John Sturgeon and a family by the name of Allsop. Last October, Sarah, the eldest of the six Allsop children, filed suit against Sturgeon, alleging that in the presence of the other children, Sturgeon stated that Sarah and her sister were 'whores and adulterers.'"

"Those words must be in the legislative statute," I interrupted.

"Yes, they are," he replied.

"An attack on a woman's virtue?"

"Indeed it is!"

"Sarah Allsop has retained Anthony Thornton and your friend Usher Linder as her attorneys."

"And who will be the counsel for the defense?"

"It's Orlando Ficklin, who has requested that you join him in defending Sturgeon."

"Let him know that I want to learn more about it, but that I'm inclined to offer him my services. This one, and that other one where the fellow wanted to shoot his daughter and son-in-law's dog, will pay the rent."

Billy gathered up the papers from the Allsop and Sturgeon file, placed them back into the folder, and tossed it onto the table. When the file landed, it caused a letter nearby to fall onto the floor.

"Oh my goodness," he said, picking up the envelope, "this arrived the other day, and I forgot about it."

I had not risen from the couch, and he brought the letter over to me. It was from Kentucky. When I looked at it more carefully, I recognized the handwriting.

"This is from Old Buster in Lexington."

I tore it open and began to read.

Friend Lincoln,

I enjoyed meeting with you when you were here.

I hope you and Mrs. Lincoln arrived home safely and that young Edward's health is improving.

We have completed the documents on Robert Todd's estate. I will mail them to Mrs. Lincoln for her signature. She can return them to me at her convenience.

It is my sad and regrettable duty to convey to you and Mrs. Lincoln some very difficult news. Yesterday, Elizabeth Porter Parker, Mrs. Lincoln's grandmother, died in her sleep. It appears that she died peacefully. In all likelihood, after eighty years, her heart simply gave out. As she had been in her usual good spirits, there was no indication of declining health. We will keep you apprised of the arrangements.

By the terms of her will, her slaves will be freed, but this news will not be well received in Lexington.

I regret being the bearer of sad news, but I'd rather you hear it directly from me.

Cordially,

George Robertson

"Oh William, how cruel," I said looking over at Billy. "First her father's death and now this—Grandmother Parker has died. I am not sure she can take any more."

I rose from the couch, picked up my hat, and walked out the door.

The snow was still falling. Though I was bundled against it, the cold pierced through my muffler and coat. My thoughts turned to the wretched task awaiting me, and I grew oblivious to my surroundings.

How could I tell Molly about the death of her grandmother? She was still grieving for her father. Now she had to face a loss of equal magnitude. It would be so difficult for her. How could I gently give her this news?

As I approached our house, my muscles tightened, and I clenched my jaw. My boots felt heavier as I climbed the steps to our front door.

When I pounded my boots against the top step to remove the mud, the door flew open, and Bobby, his face beaming with joy, asked, "Papa, will you come play with me?"

Delivered from the sadness I was feeling, I replied, "Of course, my little man, I'd be delighted to play with you."

Bobby led me into the sitting room.

"I've been playing with the stereoscope. Do you want to see how it works?

"I do."

He placed a paper card with side-by-side pictures of a waterfall into the machine.

Drawing himself up to the two eyepieces, he peered in and cried, "Oh, it's so beautiful, Papa, you have to see this."

I crouched down and viewed the scene. I did not have to pretend excitement. The flat images took on another dimension and came alive in color and detail. It was as if water were flowing through the machine.

"Bobby, how does it do this?"

"I don't know, Papa, it's just magic!"

We continued to insert cards into the device, and each time we expressed our sense of wonder and enjoyment. I was tempted to tell him how it worked, but I did not want to spoil his enchantment.

I flopped down on the floor, which was the signal for us to wrestle, but, as Bobby sat on the carpet, his face turned serious, and he asked, "Papa, why is Eddie so sick?"

"We don't know, my lad, but we do know that each time he is sick, the next day he seems to get better."

"Is something bad going to happen to him this time?"

"Oh child, no one can know, but the doctor is doing all he can."

We both heard footsteps and the rustling of a dress. Molly emerged from the door next to the table with the stereoscope. She barely tolerated her boys and her husband rolling around on her sitting room floor, and she looked at us with mild annoyance.

As I rose and greeted her, our eyes met, and she backed away, crying out, "Something terrible has happened. I can see it in your face."

I could not disguise my feelings from Molly. I had no choice. I had to tell her.

"Robertson has written me from Lexington. Grandmother Parker has died in her sleep."

She cried out again and collapsed onto one of the chairs by the fireplace. While she convulsed and heaved with sob after sob, Bobby and I tried to comfort her. She hugged Bobby closely, and I stretched my arms around them both. Ever so gradually the first waves of shock and grief eased, and we helped her up the stairs to her bedroom. We placed a blanket over her, as she continued to sob.

There was nothing more we could do. Bobby took my hand and led me into the tiny bedroom he shared with Eddie.

There, in a small bed, just large enough to hold an almost four-year-old boy, his brother Eddie was sleeping peacefully.

"He's stopped coughing," Bobby whispered excitedly.

"That's a good sign," I said softly.

For seven weeks, Eddie's little body had been wracked with fever, coughing, and chills, but at rest in his bed, his angelic face, momentarily freed from the ravages of illness, peered upward toward Bobby and me.

Sleeping peacefully was our little Eddie whom we all dearly loved: little Eddie whom Bobby and I hauled around the neighborhood in our wagon. How delighted he was when a dog stopped to sniff him and lick his face. Here was little Eddie whom I carried on my shoulders all around Springfield. We stopped to talk with a friend, and Eddie joined in when he learned to speak. This was our Eddie who cried so loudly that a neighbor came out and asked if everything was all right. "Yes," I replied, "it's just that I have only three walnuts and both he and Bobby want two." This was our little Eddie who loved cats and understood their ways. He was our little Eddie whose eyes, Molly told me, brightened at the mention of my name when I was away.

Bobby continued to hold my hand, and he asked faintly, "Papa, do you remember when Eddie tried to save the kitten?"

"I do," I said. "Your mother wrote me about it."

"I brought it home," he said proudly, "but Eddie fed it and gave it water and wanted to keep it."

It was a charming story with a sad ending. Molly's stepmother told the boys to get rid of it, and Eddie was heartbroken.

In the early evening, we received our daily visit from our brother-in-law, Dr. William Wallace. Wallace was a kindly man who had delivered both the boys and attended each of us through our sicknesses. He was much loved in Springfield, and many families had a story of how he saved someone from serious illness.

He looked over at Molly, who was pale and silent.

"Brother Lincoln and Sister Mary," he said heartily, "how is he today?"

Neither of us said anything, and the pause continued.

Finally I said, "He's resting quietly. Bobby is keeping watch over him."

"Well, let's go upstairs and have a look."

We led him to the boys' bedroom, and Bobby looked up at us with concern.

The labored breathing had returned. The little boy was gasping for breath. It sounded as if he was suffocating.

Dr. Wallace leaned down and placed his stethoscope on Eddie's chest, listened carefully to his heart and lungs, and then placed his hand on Eddie's forehead.

He stepped away from the bed, turned toward us, and spoke slowly, "The fever has returned, his breathing is irregular, and his heart is weakening. There is one last medicine we can try. I'll write out the prescription for you before I leave. There is still a sliver of hope."

Molly began to weep, lowered her head, and placed her hands over her face.

I took her hand and gave her a slight tug. She followed me willingly into her bedroom, where she sank onto the bed. I told Bobby to stay with his mother until she was asleep.

Dr. Wallace and I descended the staircase, and I led him out the front door.

When we stood on the top of the steps, he paused and put his arm on my shoulder.

"Brother," he said, "you must prepare your wife. He will die in the next day or two."

I put my hands over my face in disbelief.

"There is no hope?"

"None. His little body has fought it for almost two months. The cruelty is that there were days when he appeared to be recovering. Sometimes it happens, but not when it has gone on this long."

My tears gave way to heaving sobs, and I leaned toward the doctor, who held me in his arms.

That night after everyone was asleep, I tossed for several hours. When I couldn't sleep, I sometimes walked through the empty streets of Springfield. I arose and dressed in warm clothes.

I pulled my heavy coat over my shoulders, wrapped my neck with a muffler, and extended my fingers into a pair of thick winter gloves. I found the woolen winter hat Molly had crocheted for me and tugged it over my head. As I opened the door and descended the front steps, I was greeted by a cutting wind. There was no moon, and the darkness smothered me with its enveloping arms. As I walked up Eighth Street, past the Dean, the Lyon, and the Beedle houses, I could hear the tree limbs knocking against each other, and when I looked up, I could see them swaying fiercely in the unrelenting wind.

The unsettled mood of the elements matched my despair at the thought of losing our little boy. I was haunted by the thought that I had been away for most of his illness, away from our dying Eddie.

Walking west on Adams, I was buffeted by the blasts of the incoming storm. The snow began in sweeps of small flakes. When I reached the town square, I looked up hoping to see the familiar silhouette of the State Capitol.

Like me, it was wrapped in a shroud of darkness.

I could go no farther. I crumpled onto a nearby bench. The wind moaned and howled as it ate into me. A wave of heavier snow accompanied it.

I cried out into the night, "How can you take him from us? Why do you take the gentle ones? Freeze me into death and darkness. Take me and not him."

I must have stumbled home. I have no recollection of it. As darkness began to lift, Molly found me collapsed on the floor in front of our fireplace.

"Husband, you must come upstairs," she insisted.

On his cot in Bobby's room lay little Eddie. He was in a coma. His breathing was deeply labored, and his throat rattled.

I gently lifted Eddie and carried him to our bed, where Molly and I lay down beside him. We comforted him as best we could. I held him in my lap while Molly cradled his head on her chest.

The rattling eased away, his breathing ceased, and he was gone.

Chapter 3

I Think I Do

When I opened the office door, Billy was sitting at the table reading the morning newspapers. I walked over to the window, rested my hat on the bookshelf nearby, and then sank down onto the couch. After taking two bites out of an apple for breakfast, I stretched out, crossed my arms, and stared up at the ceiling.

After several minutes, Billy rose and went to the door. He pulled the curtain across the window, stepped outside, and locked the door so I wouldn't be disturbed. I could hear his steps receding down the hallway.

I tried to lose myself in sleep, but my thoughts intruded, one in particular. I could not keep the image of that helpless little boy from flickering through my mind. How could it have been God's will to take him? I could not agree with James Smith, the pastor who buried Eddie, when he counseled Molly and me to accept Eddie's death as part of God's plan.

My thoughts turned to Molly. For days, she kept to herself in her bedroom, crying ceaselessly and refusing to eat. It was I who told her, "Eat, Molly, for we must live." Dr. Smith met with us regularly, and gradually, she derived some comfort from his visits.

While I knew I must live, I felt that if we should be the parents of twenty children, I would always remember this one.

I had grown used to my melancholy. That didn't make it any easier when it crept in because of a memory or an event. It took hold of me and kept me in its grasp, but I knew that eventually it would ease and allow me to continue with my life. Walking through the fields and woods that bordered Springfield and through the city's streets at night helped me live with it. The hearty fellowship of men and their affairs called to me. If I could laugh and make others laugh, I felt more at home in this world from which I sometimes felt apart. These sunnier thoughts allowed me to nod off and rest.

Billy tapped lightly on the door. I awoke, rubbed and rolled my palms over my eyes, relaxed and stretched, and then walked over to the door to open it for him.

I greeted him and asked, "How long has it been, William?"

"Not quite two hours," he said as he entered the office.

We sat down at the table. Easing myself back into our daily chores, I asked him about our most pressing cases.

"Where are we on the waterwheel patent case?"

"Parker versus Hoyt?"

"Yes," I responded.

"The wheels of justice are grinding slowly on that one," he explained. "It is moving toward a trial, probably in the U.S. Circuit Court of Chicago in several months. Is there anything you want me to find out?"

"I don't think so. I'm well versed in the principles of the reaction percussion waterwheel. I was almost killed next to one."

"When the horse kicked you in the head?"

"The very same. You've had to listen to my stories for so long, and now you do me the kindness of remembering one."

When we finished reviewing Parker versus Hoyt, he asked me, "Have you heard what Douglas has done?"

"I have," I replied.

I had read the articles from Washington in the *Illinois Daily Journal* and the *Illinois State Register* the night before. They were praising Douglas for stitching together the pieces of a compromise that had eluded Henry Clay.

The Missouri Compromise had eased southern fears of an imbalance in Congress—which could threaten the existence of slavery. Sectional conflict receded until 1848, when we acquired territory from Mexico as the spoils of war. For months Congress argued over the Wilmot Proviso that would have kept slavery out of this territory. It failed to pass, but the debate over slavery had resumed. It remained unresolved. Conflicting voices from proponents of abolition and secession grew stronger. Congress had to deal with the slavery agitation that was pulling the country apart.

Henry Clay tried to combine individual measures for California statehood, the border of Texas, governments for the Utah and New Mexico territories, abolition of the slave trade in Washington, DC, and a stronger fugitive slave law into an omnibus bill. It did not pass.

Clay returned to Kentucky, and Douglas took charge. He recognized there was a group of senators who would vote for all the legislation. If he could combine that group with southern votes for some of the measures and northern votes for the others, he could secure passage for each one. It was a brilliant strategy that he executed perfectly.

"What do today's newspapers say about him?" I asked.

"That he has defused the sectional tension over slavery that has been building for the past few years."

"And he is the hero of the age?" I asked.

"Yes, that is what they are calling him."

What separated the Judge from the rest of us was the swiftness of his political rise. While I was toiling through four terms in the state legislature, he held four Illinois state offices, became the register of the Federal Land Office in Springfield, and won election to Congress in 1843. His success in Congress brought him re-election and recognition as the leading Democrat in Illinois. In his two terms in the House, Douglas was deeply involved in the annexation of Texas and settling the Oregon territorial dispute with Great Britain—which led to his appointment as chairman of the Committee on Territories. In my one congressional term, I served on the Committee on the Post Office and Post Roads.

In 1838, when Douglas ran against my law partner, John Todd Stuart, for a seat in Congress, he lost the election by 36 votes. It was his only defeat. Douglas's response to his loss was to run again and win. I lost my first race for the state legislature, four elections representing the Whig candidate as an elector, and was not renominated for my congressional seat. Most recently I was passed over by the Taylor administration as a candidate for commissioner of the National Land Office. With me, the race of ambition had been a failure—a flat failure; with him it had been one of splendid success.

It was no surprise when Douglas won election to the United States Senate in 1847 at the age of 33. From the start he became an influential senator. The lions of the Senate, Henry Clay, Daniel Webster, and John C. Calhoun, were in the twilight of their lives, and Douglas was the rising star.

Perhaps it was his youth, perhaps it was his boundless energy or the force of his personality and personal magnetism, but underneath it all was a masterful politician. His instincts were unerring, and he could patch fragmented groups together into working coalitions.

He was being encouraged to run for president. After one term in Congress, my political career was over. I was in the Judge's shadow, and it was hard not to envy his success.

We tidied up several law cases, and by then it was time to eat. Billy brought his dinner to the office, and sometimes I joined him, but more often I walked back to our home for the meal Molly prepared for Bobby and me.

As I walked home for dinner, my thoughts turned to Molly. She had become more temperamental in the last few months. It was behavior for which she was known in her family and among her friends before we met, and it continued from time to time during our marriage, but, since the loss of Eddie, it had become more pronounced.

There was a flash of it when we were first married and living at the Globe Tavern. Breakfast was served at eight o'clock, and no one could eat until everyone was seated. Molly was continually late, so one morning I said to her in a soft voice, "Dearest, you arc trying these people's patience. Couldn't you please be on time?" She frowned at me, picked up her cup of coffee, and threw it in my face.

Later in our marriage, when I returned home after a particularly difficult trial, I greeted Molly, who was preparing supper in the kitchen. I eased into my comfortable chair by the fireplace and began reading the day's newspapers.

From the kitchen, I heard a loud call; "Mr. Lincoln, don't let the fire go out!"

I looked at the fire, which seemed just fine, and did not reply.

"Mr. Lincoln, don't let the fire go out," came the second call. I looked over at the fire, and while it was starting to flicker, it wasn't in imminent danger of expiring.

I have to admit, I did not hear the third call.

What I did hear was the irate cry of my angry wife, and the smash of a hard object into my face. While I pressed my handkerchief onto my bloody nose, I looked down to see the ashes in the fireplace and a large piece of firewood on the floor. The next day I went to the office with plasters on my face, and Billy was good enough not to ask about them.

I could never be sure what awaited me at home.

I walked past the Carrigan home, and there, on the left side of the street, was our house. Bob greeted me joyfully when I walked into the family parlor. Although he too had grieved for Eddie, he was now himself again.

"Papa, papa," he cried, "there's a strange, mean dog in the neighborhood, and he almost bit me. He's big and black, and I had to run away from him."

"Are you all right?"

"Yes, but I'm not going outside until he's gone."

"I didn't see him on my way home. Let's have our dinner and then see if he's still gone."

"Mama's happy today," he told me gaily, and then he skipped off to the kitchen to tell Molly I was home for our meal.

From around the corner, Molly appeared wearing an apron. She looked as young and rosy as I first remembered her. For some reason, her face had momentarily shed the heavy pallor of grief. She bounded toward me and gave me a warm hug.

She asked impishly, "What happens in the first days of winter?"

This was an odd question, but I replied, "It's almost always cold, and sometimes it snows."

"Yes, that's it. You're on the right track. But what else happens that time of year?"

"It's the holidays and we celebrate with friends."

"Yes, but there's something else we celebrate. What is it?"

I was hopelessly confused, but it came to me.

"I suppose that since Dr. Smith has captured your heart, we will pay some attention to Christmas."

"Yes, yes, but what do we celebrate at Christmas?"

"Well, you may celebrate it, but I remain dubious."

"You are such a blockhead! The Virgin Mary gives birth to the baby Jesus."

"I know that. It's just that I don't believe it."

She gave me as loving a look as I could recall, and then it struck like lightning.

"You will have a child near Christmastime!"

For her, it was as if all the unhappiness of the last year had lifted. She was once again the Molly whom I loved—my companion and my mate. In our embrace, we forgot the cares of the world and were, once again, joyful for all we had lived through together.

"If he is a boy, we will name him William Wallace Lincoln, after our brother-in-law."

"And if she is a girl, we will name her for you."

As the fall of 1850 turned into an early winter, Molly and I found comfort sitting beside our warm and cozy fireplace. While Bobby worked on a wooden jigsaw puzzle on the carpet near the fire, Molly and I read separately and sometimes to each other.

She read the latest Dickens novel, and I read the newspapers aloud softly to myself so I wouldn't disturb her. It was a custom we observed from time to time, but after the loss of Eddie and with Molly's pregnancy, we practiced it more regularly, mostly in the evening. When she came to a particularly exciting passage, she read it to me, and I would lower the paper and listen to the ornate, flowing language. Molly read it with the lively expression an actress might use in a dramatic moment onstage. I didn't care much for novels, but Molly had an ear for passages that begged to be read aloud. Sometimes she would ask me to read from her novel, and I obliged.

One evening I came home with a copy of one of Billy's abolitionist publications, *The National Era*, because he had started reading the first segments of a story called *Uncle Tom's Cabin* by a woman named Harriet Beecher Stowe. Mrs. Stowe wrote it to be a portrait of slavery. I had little use for such a thing, but Billy said it was something Molly might enjoy.

Having just finished *David Copperfield*, and in despair until the next Dickens arrived, she welcomed this new story. That night she devoured the first five chapters.

"Husband," she said excitedly, "it starts in Kentucky where you grew up. To save his farm, Mr. Shelby must sell two of his slaves, the faithful, kindly Tom and the boy

Harry, who is the son of Eliza, Mrs. Shelby's maid. He has to sell them to the slave trader Haley. Mr. Shelby deceives his wife, but she finds out what he has done. This is what she says to him.

"'This is God's curse on slavery!—a bitter, bitter, most accursed thing!—a curse to the master and a curse to the slave! I was a fool to think I could make anything good of such a deadly evil. It is a sin to hold a slave under laws like ours,—I always felt it was,—I always thought so when I was a girl,—I thought so still more after I joined the church; but I thought I could gild it over,—I thought, by kindness, and care, and instruction, I could make the condition of my slaves better than freedom—fool that I was!'"

Molly added, "And at the end of the chapter, Eliza has decided to run off with her little Harry."

I had to admit this sounded like a cracking good story.

"I look forward to hearing more of this," I said to her. "Billy gets a copy of it each month, and I'll bring it home when he's done with it."

On the morning of December 21, 1850, when the air was brisk and the snow glistened in the sparkling sunlight and the sky was royal blue, Dr. William Wallace attended Molly as she gave birth to William Wallace Lincoln. We decided we would call him Willie.

Molly looked up at Dr. Wallace and me, and said, "We are blessed beyond measure this Christmas."

We were overwhelmed with joy. After all she had lived through in the past year—the loss of her father, her grandmother, and Eddie—Willie's birth brought renewal and purpose. She was a loving mother, and she devoted herself to our new arrival. The heavy clouds that hovered over Bobby dispersed, and he was delighted at the prospect of having a new playmate. He ran around the neighborhood announcing the birth of his younger brother.

I was awed by life's cycle. After dreadful loss, we were blessed with new life. Perhaps the joy was even greater because of the depth of the loss. I had sworn to myself that I would never forget Eddie's angelic face or his struggle and suffering, but I was open to the love I felt for Willie. It was hard to experience such a range of feelings, but then many of our family and friends had lost a child and then welcomed another.

With a happiness we had not known for months, we celebrated Christmas and the New Year.

During the first week in January, a letter arrived for me in the morning while I was at the office. When we were sitting together in the family parlor that evening, Molly gave it to me and said, "I think it's from your stepbrother John."

I wondered why I would be hearing from John D. Johnston. My stepbrother was a ne'er do well who often besieged me with requests for money. I opened the letter, which was short.

Dear Brother,

I hope you are well, but Father is very low and will hardly recover. You came last time and he saw it through. Dennis, Elizabeth, and Harriet are here. We are not sure this time will not be different.

Your brother,

John D.

"What does it say?" Molly asked.

"My father may be dying. This happened once before."

"Does he ask you to come?"

"Yes, although my brother does not say so, it is my father's wish."

"Will you go see him?"

I turned away and looked at the fire. It had almost gone out.

"I don't know," I said indifferently.

"I am so saddened for you."

"There is nothing you can do."

That evening, when Molly and Bobby were asleep, I sat at the desk in my bedroom trying to write a letter to John D.

It was a small desk, which I had placed in the corner of the room so that I could look out the window facing west. Late in the afternoon I could see the sun setting, but when I worked there at night, the only light was from the moon and the candle that flickered in the darkness.

I loved this old piece of furniture. Molly found it for me because she thought the eight cubbyholes directly behind the level writing surface could hold the drafts of letters, speeches, and law briefs. The candleholder sat on the top shelf. Once, when one of the legs broke, Molly put it out on the street for removal. One of our neighbors fixed it and left it near the front steps. I never knew who, so I was not able to thank him. Although it was a tiny desk for a large man, it served its purpose. I was a light sleeper, if I slept at all, and many nights found me at work in this corner.

Now, as my father lay dying and I tried to write my stepbrother, I was struck by the thought that this little desk reminded me of the pieces my father had constructed when he was building furniture. It was what he most loved doing.

I could not think of my father, though, without remembering the tension that always existed between us. We tried to deflect it, but it was too deep to deny. He just didn't understand who I was or who I wanted to become. He did not want me to read, to learn, or to better myself. He took it as an affront to himself. He stood for everything I did not want to be. He felt that in trying to find my own path, I was rejecting him. My stepmother Sally tried, but there could be no reconciliation between us. I'd had to escape from him.

The words did not come easily, but eventually I wrote what I could.

Dear Brother,

I am deeply saddened to learn of Father's illness, but my business is such that I could hardly leave home now.

I sincerely hope Father may yet recover his health; but at all events tell him to remember to call upon and confide in, our great, and good, and merciful Maker; who will not turn away from him in any extremity. He notes the fall of a sparrow, and numbers the hairs of our heads; and He will not forget the dying man, who puts his trust in Him. Say to him that if we could meet now, it is doubtful whether it would not be more painful than pleasant; but that if it be his lot to go now, he will soon have a joyous meeting with many loved ones gone before; and where the rest of us, through the help of God, hope ere long to join them.

Write me again when you receive this.

Affectionately,

A. Lincoln

On January 17, 1851, Father died. I did not attend his funeral.

Molly and I continued to read *Uncle Tom's Cabin* to each other by the fireplace in our family parlor. In the segments Billy gave us, the slave trader Haley rides after Eliza and Harry hoping to capture them. Eliza eludes him, but, carrying Harry, she has to leap across the spring ice chunks in the Ohio River to reach safety on the other side.

I read part of this scene to Molly. "The huge green fragment of ice on which she alighted pitched and creaked as her weight came on it, but she stayed there not a moment. With wild cries and desperate energy she leaped to another and still another cake;—stumbling—leaping—slipping—springing upwards again! Her shoes are gone, her stockings cut from her feet—while blood marked every step . . . "

Haley employs the vile slave catcher Tom Loker to track down Eliza. Haley tells Loker he can keep Eliza but must bring him the boy.

When we reached this part, Molly read what he might do to Eliza. Talking to Haley, Loker says, " . . . If she's got a young un to be sold, I jest walks up and puts my fist to her face, and says, 'Look here, now, if you give me one word out of your head, I'll smash yer face in. I won't hear one word—not the beginning of a word.' I says to 'em, 'This yer young un's mine, and not yours, and you've no kind o' business with it. I'm going to sell it, first chance; mind, you don't cut up none o' yer shines about it, or I'll make ye wish ye'd never been born.'"

In subsequent chapters, Mrs. Stowe tells Tom's story. Haley returns to the Shelby farm to fetch Tom, tear him from his family, and take him to New Orleans, where he will most likely be sold to a hard and cruel owner.

Molly and I were overcome by the power of Mrs. Stowe's story. I wondered how anyone could read it and still believe that negroes were not human beings. Although this portrait of slavery appeared in a novel, Mrs. Stowe was said to be preparing a publication with the letters, diaries, and newspaper articles she used to write her book.

The following morning, I walked over to Sixth Street and then up to the capitol building. I wanted to stop by the law library to check on a small detail that could make a difference in one of our cases.

As I climbed the stairs to the front door, I saw an unmistakable figure crouched over on the bench to the left of the entrance. He was a short man with his hands over the sides of his head, exposing a large crop of dark brown hair. Dressed in a sharply tailored black suit, he appeared quite distracted. I came closer and took a second look to be sure, but there was no doubt.

"Judge," I called to him, "what are you doing here?"

My greeting caused him to focus, and he addressed me warmly.

"Why, Mr. Lincoln, what an unexpected pleasure!"

"And for me as well," I replied, "but that does not answer my question."

"Alas, my dear friend, I am interrupting my colloquies with constituents to settle a frivolous lawsuit."

"Judge," I said while peering down at him, "some of them are frivolous and some of them ain't."

"A fine point, but this one is very frivolous indeed! One of your distant Edwards relations has filed a claim to the land I bought here years ago. Can you imagine that? It's something that might have happened thirty years ago. But let's not be bothered by it. 'For God's sake, sit down next to me upon this bench, and tell sad stories of the death of kings.'"

I sat down next to him on the bench and looked out over the park to the row of buildings on Adams Street. My mood turned mellow.

"Judge, do you remember when we performed the scene from *A Midsummer Night's Dream* for the Springfield Mechanics Union?"

"Indeed I do. We were worse than any mechanicals who've ever performed upon the boards."

"Give us a few of Bottom's lines."

He looked up, cleared his throat, and then bellowed in that melodious, unmistakable voice, "Let me play the lion too. I will roar that I will do any man's heart good to hear me. I will roar that I will make the Duke say, 'Let him roar again; let him roar again.'"

His face brightened as he concluded, and then he asked, "Do you remember what Bottom says at the end of the scene?"

I looked at him and started laughing.

"No, no, my friend, too early! You must listen carefully to what he says. 'We will meet, and there we may rehearse most obscenely and courageously.'"

He could barely finish the line before convulsing with spasms of continuing laughter. It was contagious. I was laughing at both Bottom's line and the Judge's response to it. We couldn't stop laughing hilariously at both the Judge's recitation and at each other. When one of us stopped laughing, the other started again.

"Oh, Judge, this is too rich, too rich."

Gradually we slipped back into our normal roles.

He looked at me thoughtfully and said, "I heard that you and Mrs. Lincoln lost one of your boys. My condolences. Have you recovered, and how is Mrs. Lincoln?"

I looked out once more over the park and choked back my feelings.

"Neither of us has recovered. We go about our lives, and that helps, but it has stayed with us. Willie's birth this past Christmas has helped us focus on what is to come."

I paused and then asked him, "And your wife and sons? Are they well?"

He replied, "Martha is still frail, but she and the boys are with her family in North Carolina while I am in Washington. She can rest, and the boys are always into something. There's plenty for them to do down there."

Our conversation eased and we sat quietly.

"Don't you find it a curious coincidence," I asked him, "that we both married women from slaveholding families?"

He gave me an odd look.

"No, that hadn't occurred to me," he replied. "I'd say the coincidence is we both married money. Not a bad idea, my friend."

I turned to look at him directly, and said, "Judge, you are the talk of Washington. Calhoun is dead, Clay is ill, and Webster is in decline. You are the heir apparent."

"Not so fast, my friend, Clay put together the omnibus bill. When it failed, I added the finishing touches. He was the heart of it."

"But the newspapers are saluting you as the hero of the age."

"As well I might be if it weren't for this damned slavery agitation."

"Yes, that is the flaw," I replied. "You and Clay had to agree to the Fugitive Slave Act. It's the piece that could cause the whole thing to topple. It has inflamed the abolitionists."

"That and this damned Stowe book that everyone's reading."

"Are you reading it?"I asked.

"Lincoln, you can't be serious. First of all, I don't read trash, and second, it's sentimental tripe that doesn't show the good of slavery. Heaven knows how a novel can turn this country upside down."

"Molly and I are reading it in the segments Billy Herndon gives us from *The National Era*."

He looked utterly aghast, and then his face softened.

"I've always known the milk of human kindness flows through you, Lincoln. I was in the legislature when you and Stone went on record about slavery—although you did point out the evils of abolition. I don't know where it comes from, other than your kindly nature, but you and I have never agreed about the negro."

"Yes, Judge, that's so."

"So this Mrs. Stowe has transformed them into human beings?"

"Yes, Judge, that's about right."

"And you see them as human?"

"The woman I saw at the slave auction in Lexington was just as human as you or I."

"Well, my friend, much as I like you, I will oppose any national policy based on that assumption. I will not see our country destroyed by those who believe the negro is entitled to the same rights as the white man. This country was founded by white men for white men. The negro is not, nor ever will be, the equal of the white man."

"So you see no moral issue in relation to the negro?"

"None."

He paused, and then he asked, "And you, Mr. Lincoln?"

"I think I do," I replied.

Chapter 4

And They Have the Same Basic Rights as the White Man

Most of my law cases were mundane, but once in a while came a case that fully engaged me. Such a case was *Parker v. Hoyt*.

In October 1829, Zebulon Parker obtained a patent for his invention utilizing the basic principles of a reaction percussion water wheel. In 1848, when Parker learned of Charles Hoyt's invention using the same principles, he sued Hoyt for patent infringement. After much legal maneuvering, the case was tried in the U.S. Circuit Court, District of Illinois in Chicago. With my friend Grant Goodrich, a Chicago lawyer, I represented the defendant.

I took a particular interest in the case because my role was to explain how a water wheel worked. Not only did I study this carefully, but it took me back to my New Salem days when I worked for Denton Offutt at his grist and sawmill. It was the force of the water in the Sangamon River that enabled the millstones to grind the grain into flour and the saw to cut through large pieces of wood. Goodrich and I believed Parker's patent to be a sham because enforcing it would have put every mill owner in the country out of business. In fact, the infamous Parker had sued several other unsuspecting mill owners who had settled with him rather than paying legal fees.

The trial lasted two weeks. As clearly and carefully as I could, I explained the action of the water on the wheel, showing them that Hoyt had not infringed upon Parker's patent. During my elaborate and detailed presentation, I could see that the jury understood my argument and was swayed by it—or so I thought.

Goodrich and I were concerned that the judge appeared to favor the plaintiff. In his instructions to the jury, he seemed to dismiss our line of reasoning. When the jury retired, we ate lunch at a nearby tavern, and then took a walk.

The jury deliberated for over two hours in a building next to the courtroom with an open window facing the street. When we walked by, one of the jurors, who seemed sympathetic to our arguments, looked at me and held up one of his fingers. I took this to mean he was the only one holding out against the other eleven jurors. Goodrich was discouraged, but I buoyed him with a story of a juror in one of my cases in Tazewell County.

I was trying a divorce case. My client was a pretty, refined woman who was married to a grotesque, coarse man, entirely unfitted to be her husband. Though he had mistreated her, he had not been personally violent, which was required by the statute for divorce. In their deliberations, the jury wished to side with the woman but could not justify it. When they had drawn up a verdict, one juror resisted, saying, "Gentlemen, I am going to lie down to sleep, and when you get ready to give a verdict for that woman, wake me up, for before I will give a verdict against her, I will lie here until I rot and the ants carry me out of the keyhole."

Once again, my instincts were right. The jury in *Parker v. Hoyt* found for the defendant. I was deeply gratified, and I felt it one of the most important triumphs of my law career. Patent protection was essential, but it shouldn't be misapplied.

I was the holder of patent #6,469 for a device I invented to buoy vessels over shoals. It was granted to me on May 22,

1849. I believed the patent system secured to the inventor, for a limited time, the exclusive use of his invention, and thereby added to the interest of genius in the discovery and production of new and useful things.

On the evening of a frigid December day, Molly and I were sitting by the fireplace enjoying the warmth of the blazing flames. Outside the wind howled and threatened to keep us captive under wave after wave of snow. Our recent addition, Fido, a large yellow dog, lay asleep at Molly's feet. We were both thankful for Prometheus's gift to mankind.

Molly told me, "I waited for you to come home from the circuit before I read any further in *Uncle Tom's Cabin.*"

"It slipped my mind to have Billy bring over the issues of the *National Era* while I was away,"

"I wouldn't have read ahead without you."

"By now Mrs. Stowe must have finished it."

"Yes, she did, and it has been published as a book. Simeon Francis has loaned me his copy."

"We'll have to purchase one of our own."

"It's not as easy as that. Every printing has sold out in a few days."

"But if you have Francis's book, we can read it tonight."

Molly recalled, "I think we were at the chapter where Simon Legree becomes Tom's new owner."

I put more logs on the fire, while she fetched blankets for each of us along with Francis's copy of the book.

When she returned, Molly explained, "Legree buys Tom, and he comes to hate him. He whips and beats Tom constantly."

She and I read this part of the story late into the night.

Molly read Legree's diatribe against Tom.

"'I hate him!' said Legree, 'I hate him! And isn't he MINE? Can't I do what I like with him? Who's to hinder, I wonder?' And Legree clenched his fist, and shook it, as if he had something in his hands that he could rend in pieces."

When it was my turn, I continued, "Legree drew in a long breath; and, suppressing his rage, took Tom by the arm, and approaching his face almost to his, said in a terrible voice, 'Hark 'e, Tom!—Ye think, 'cause I've let you off before, I don't mean what I say; but, this time, I've made up my mind, and counted the cost. You've always stood it out agin me: now I'll conquer ye or kill ye!—one or t'other. I'll count every drop of blood there is in you, and take 'em, one by one, till ye give up.'"

When we finished the book, we were unable to speak. Molly closed her eyes and looked as if she were in a trance.

Finally I broke the silence.

"She has made them real. It destroys the basic argument for slavery: that they are not human beings and can be bought and sold like property."

"Or that they are simple beings and cannot exist without slavery," said Molly.

"And they have the same basic rights as the white man," I added.

The next morning, I trudged through the snow to our office. When I arrived, Billy had prepared our coffee. I hung my coat on a peg and put my hat on the table. Several letters and legal papers fell out of it. I ignored them and reclined on the sofa.

"What do the newspapers tell us this morning, Billy?" I asked.

"Not much, Lincoln," he replied.

"Nothing about Douglas and the Nebraska territory?"

"Nothing."

"Is that letter on the table for me?" I asked.

"No, it's for me from Theodore Parker."

I gave him a skeptical look, and then said, "Ah, another epistle to push me toward abolition?"

He picked up the letter, fumbled with it for a moment, looked up at me, and began to read.

"Friend Herndon,

Boston is shaken by the news which I relay to you.

In Stafford County, Virginia, a slave named Anthony Burns escaped from a planter to whom he'd been hired out by his owner. Burns fled to Richmond and stowed away on a ship to Boston.

Burns began a life in freedom, but a few months later, he wrote a letter to his brother in Virginia. By mistake, it reached his owner. In the letter Burns informed his brother of his location in Boston.

The owner rushed to Boston and had Burns arrested under the damnable Fugitive Slave Act. The federal commissioner, appointed under that heinous statute, held a rendition trial by which the owner expected to recover his 'property.'

A crowd of 2,000 abolitionists, free negroes, and other citizens of Boston, surrounded the jail to protest for Burns's release. I was among them. A small group smashed in the door of the jail with a large beam, but was repulsed. In the melee a federal deputy was killed.

President Pierce sent soldiers and artillery to keep the peace. Certain that Burns would not go free, Pierce sent a federal ship to return him to his owner in Virginia.

Yesterday, Burns was convicted of being a fugitive slave. Hours later, the state militia cleared the way through 50,000 angry Bostonians who lined the streets to protest his transfer from the jail to the ship.

With my own eyes I saw the negro man, Anthony Burns, being led through the streets of Boston in shackles.

My friend, we abolitionists must unite in our hatred of slavery. The time has come for us to stand up and stand together for its abolition. If we are seen as extremists, that is because the problem requires an extreme solution. We must protest and use the courts to further our just cause. This horrid Fugitive Slave Act must be repealed. The hour of deliverance is coming. I hope you will stand with us as we continue our crusade of freedom for all.

Regards,

Your friend,

Theo. Parker"

When Billy finished reading the letter, we were both silent for a while. I think he was waiting to hear what I would say, and finally I spoke.

"Those are frightening events, Billy. This seems to happen in Boston. The Boston Massacre set our revolution in motion. The Fugitive Slave Act was a tragic mistake. If Judge Douglas thought it would heal our divide, he was wrong. Parker is right—it must be repealed, but that is not likely. Unless that happens, it is the law, and we must obey it."

"Lincoln, I don't think it will be possible to compromise on the slavery issue."

We both sat quietly for a few moments, and then I said, "Billy, you may be right, but we can't let the abolitionists lead us into a civil war. My only disagreement with you is how to end slavery. We must do it without causing a war."

I got up and moved toward the door, but I turned to him and said, "I need to talk to someone who can help me clear my head, and from whom I can also get a haircut."

William Florville was born in Haiti in 1806. Fifteen years later, he and his godmother immigrated to Baltimore. There he went to a Catholic school and was apprenticed to a barber. It was a trade he practiced for life. After living briefly in New Orleans and St. Louis, he decided to move to Illinois. As a free negro, he believed it best to become a resident of a free state.

I first met him when he appeared one day in New Salem. He was on his way to Springfield to open a barber shop. We became instant friends, and I helped him get started. Although my hair was always a mess, Billy became my barber. He straightened it out for a week or so, and then it reverted to its normal state. At least it was a bit shorter.

Billy became a fixture in Springfield, and we all knew him as Billy the barber. He was a capable business owner and a savvy investor. Real estate in Springfield was his specialty. He owned all the houses on Washington Street between Eighth and Ninth Streets. I represented him in several title suits.

He put an advertisement for his services in the *Illinois State Journal*.

WM. FLORVILLE
BARBER & HAIR-DRESSER
Billy will always be found on the spot,
With razors keen and water smoking hot:
He'll clip and dress your hair, and shave with ease
And leave no effort slack his friends to please.
His shop is north-west of the public square,
Just below the office of the Mayor;
Stranger or friends may always find him there,
Ready to shave them well or cut their hair.
On Sunday, until 9 o'clock he'll shave,
And then to church he'll go, his soul to save.
To his old customers, for favors past,
His gratitude, indeed, will ever last;
He hopes by attention and efforts rare,
A part of public patronage to share.

He became a close friend.

His shop was not only for haircuts, but it also became a gathering spot for conversations about local affairs and national politics. Sometimes I dropped over in the evening for an impromptu concert with Billy playing the violin.

After I left the office, I walked over to Billy's shop. I opened the door expecting to see the normal crowd of local politicians, but I was surprised to find no one except my friend.

He greeted me heartily.

"Mr. Lincoln, what a pleasure. I wondered if you might stop by today."

He spoke with a lilt in his voice dating back to his youth in Haiti.

"To what do I owe your auspicious visit to my emporium?" he continued.

"To my need for your tonsorial services, your sage counsel on a possible land transaction, and your discerning assessment of the political winds in the state of Illinois," I replied.

A perplexed expression rippled across his face, but it was quickly followed by a smile.

"Let's begin with your tonsorial needs, and then we'll proceed to the others. What will it be?"

"A shave and a shearing," I answered, "but I have little confidence it will do any good."

"Mr. Lincoln, we have been down this road before. Your hair is thick, stiff, and tangled. That's its natural form. Whatever shape we try to give it vanishes as it grows. It's simply whether you like it longer or shorter."

"Let's go for our usual trim."

He started with a shave. I was very quiet as he wielded the blade with a sure and masterful touch. When he toweled off my face and began the hair cutting, we could converse again.

We discussed the pros and cons of the property in which I was interested. He leaned against purchasing it, and I decided to take his advice. We then turned to politics.

"Do you think Douglas is getting out of touch with his constituents back here in Illinois?" I asked him.

He seemed momentarily stunned and pulled back from his chair. His face was somber.

"You haven't heard?" he asked.

"Heard what?"

"The sad news from Washington."

"No, I haven't. So that's why no one is in here today?"

"Yes, I expect so, but I would have thought you would be one of the first to hear."

"Out with it, Billy, what has happened?"

"Judge Douglas's wife died giving birth to a child. The baby is very weak and not expected to live."

I stared blankly at him and then cried, "Oh, my Lord, what an unspeakable tragedy!"

I crumpled forward, lowering my head.

Neither of us could pull ourselves together, until I asked, "How did you learn this? When did you hear it?"

"Mr. Trumbull came in this morning and told me. His wife is in Washington, and she sent him a letter the minute she heard it herself."

"Molly must know by now. She and Julia have always been very close."

"I don't much cotton to the Judge, but we've always been friendly," said Billy.

"I've had my differences with him too, but right now they seem mighty small. The Judge was plenty picky about getting married, but he'd found one who was lovely and rich, and who could put up with him. Poor Molly has to put up with me without the riches."

"Yes, Mr. Lincoln, you better run along home now and tell her before someone else does."

Molly had received a letter from Julia Trumbull, and she was deeply saddened for the Judge.

We comforted each other, ate a simple lunch, and went for a walk through the woods north of Springfield. In the mid-afternoon, we reached the Sangamon River.

"It was near here that we decided to marry," she said softly.

"Yes," I said, "I still have you, while the Judge is bereft of joy and happiness."

"Let us rejoice for what we have and wish the poor man some solace and peace."

Late that night, I was working at the desk in my bedroom. A light breeze played with branches of a large oak tree near our house. Dappling the stones and dirt on Eighth Street was the light from the three-quarter moon. A neighbor's dog barked. I started to compose a letter I had thought about all day.

Dear Judge,

Springfield, Feb. 4, 1853

I learned this morning of your unexpected and grievous loss. We have all lost loved ones, but no one can know the depth of your loss. The sorrows and sufferings of the world are now on your shoulders.

We have been friends and rivals for almost twenty years. Although we are members of different political parties, and although we have had differences on local and national issues, there is a bond between us that transcends these differences.

In that spirit, let me offer you and your sons my condolences and my assurance that you are in my thoughts during this time of grief and loss.

Mary grieves for you as well.

A. Lincoln

A month later I received the Judge's response.

Dear Lincoln,

Washington, DC, February 26, 1853

I am grateful for your letter of February 4.

As ever, your sentiments are kind and thoughtful.

Yes, we have both known loss.

My loss is magnified. The little girl to whom Martha gave birth has died as well.

The boys are bearing up as boys will do.

I have resumed my duties in the Senate, but I am distracted and low. Friends advise me to go to Europe for some months.

I am deeply appreciative of your kindness, and I wish you well in all your endeavors.

S. Douglas

Late winter turned to early spring. On April 4, 1853, we celebrated the birth of our fourth child. We were blessed with another boy. Since our first child was named after her father, Molly wanted to name our fourth boy Thomas, after my father. I agreed and, before too long, I gave him a suitable nickname. Because he had a large head and a skinny body, we called him Tad for tadpole. We felt that our blessing had come in the shadow of Judge Douglas's terrible loss, but once again we were witnessing the cycle of death and life.

On a warm late April evening, as I walked home from the office, I was particularly absorbed in my thoughts. That confounded Billy Herndon was trying to turn me into an abolitionist. His friendship with Theodore Parker had confirmed his abolitionist views—that and all the anti-slavery tracts he read in the eastern newspapers and periodicals. I was still sorting through my own thoughts on slavery, and I didn't need Billy trying to tug me his way.

I strolled on home, but as I came closer, I heard a child's screams. When I realized it was from our house, I ran quickly and then saw drops of blood on our doorsteps. I rushed through the front door and up the stairs. Bob was writhing and screaming on his bed, and Molly and Dr. Wallace were holding him down. On his right leg was a nasty wound that continued to bleed. Dr. Wallace was attempting to bandage it.

"He was bitten by that black dog," cried Molly. "It ran away before anyone could catch it or shoot it."

"Is it the same one we've seen around the neighborhood?" I asked.

"I think so, but Bob has been so upset, he can't tell us what happened."

Gradually the doctor succeeded in attaching the bandage and wrapping the leg, and Bob started to calm down. He was able to tell us he was playing with a stick, and the dog tried to rip it from him. Bob yanked the stick away, but the dog bit him on the leg.

Molly stayed with Bob, while Dr. Wallace and I went downstairs.

He seemed deeply concerned.

"Brother Lincoln," he said, "this could be very serious."

"Yes, I reckon so," I replied, but then I asked, "What should we do?"

"I don't like what we're hearing about this dog."

"It could be hydrophobia?"

"I'm afraid so. Once the symptoms appear, death follows slowly."

"There is no cure?"

"None."

"None?"

"Well, there is some nonsense about something called a madstone."

"And what is that?"

"I've heard it comes from a deer's stomach, something that can't be digested and forms into a solid object. It's about the size of a small stone, but it is actually porous. You put it on the wound to remove the poison. There's an odd ritual in using it, but no one around here does it."

"Is it a matter of time?"

"I think so. The sooner the better. We may have a month, maybe a little more or a little less."

Molly and I agreed that if there was nothing else, we should try to treat Bob with a madstone. I gave Billy Herndon the task of finding someone, and he turned up a woman in Terre Haute. It was a considerable distance, but the next day, Bob and I set out in the buggy with Old Buck. On the way back, we could stop by and visit my mama in Coles County.

As Old Buck plodded along, and Bob wanted to know what was happening, he asked me questions and listened thoughtfully to my answers.

"Papa, will I get sick?"

"Bobby, we certainly hope not, and we are doing everything we can to see that you don't. We are going on this trip to meet someone who thinks she can help you stay well."

"Papa, what's a madstone?"

"I didn't know anything about it until a few days ago. It's something that comes from the belly of a deer that our new friend will put on your leg to draw out anything harmful."

"How will it do that?"

"I don't rightly know, but we'll find out when we get there."

"Papa, will you tell me a story?"

"Yes, of course, Bobby, here's one for you.

"There was a great person in our history, a politician called Daniel Webster. Well, when Daniel was young and in school, he did something awful. The teacher wanted to hit his hand with a ruler, but when Daniel gave him his hand, it was very dirty. The teacher said to him, 'Daniel, if you will find another hand in this schoolroom as filthy as that, I will let you off this time.' Well, Daniel instantly said, 'Here it is, sir' and showed him his other hand!"

When we arrived in Terre Haute, we were able to find the woman's house easily because of the directions Billy had given us.

She lived in the rundown part of the town. Her house was decrepit on the outside and dark and cluttered inside, but the old woman, Mrs. Ingrid Hagedorn, welcomed us warmly.

"Don't mind the cats," she rasped. "They keep the mice away."

"I love cats," Bob replied. "Papa, there must be twenty of them."

She asked to see Bob's wound and unwrapped his bandage.

"Ooh, nasty, very nasty," she cooed, "full of pus, so full of pus! The little charm is just for you, my young friend."

She explained the ritual she would follow. She showed us a pail of warm milk in which the madstone was soaking. This was to make it more absorbent. Once it was ready, she would apply it to Bob's wound. If it did not adhere, he would not develop the symptoms of hydrophobia. If it did adhere, it would stay attached until it sucked out the poison. When it detached, which might take up to an hour, Mrs. Hagedorn would put it back into the warm milk. If it had done its work, it would emit a greenish fluid.

After giving us these instructions, she reached into the milk and pulled out the madstone. Though covered by a thin layer of milk, we could clearly see a vanilla-colored object with the size and shape of a small muffin. Each side had a crusty surface with small dark indentations.

Bob was seated on a rickety chair with his leg propped onto a small stool. She asked us if we were ready, and I nodded my approval. When she placed the madstone on his wound, Bob flinched momentarily. Slowly it seemed to be attaching itself to his leg. He settled down and occupied the time by asking Mrs. Hagedorn ceaseless questions about the madstone. The time passed slowly for me, but I was startled out of my trance by the noise of something clunking onto the floor.

"Ah!" cried Mrs. Hagedorn. "It has detached. I do not think we have to do it again. Now comes the real test."

She prepared the milk for our last step.

Several minutes later, she dropped the madstone into the pot with the warm milk.

We anxiously awaited the result.

Ever so gradually, the white fluid assumed a light green tint and then a deeper shade of green.

"Young fellow," crowed Mrs. Hagedorn, "the poison has been removed from your wound, and you will live to be an old man like your father!"

In November, Douglas was back in the Senate after a tour of Europe, where he was treated like a visiting head of state. He started in London, where he did not meet Queen Victoria because he refused to wear "court dress." He then headed east to Constantinople, circled back to Florence and Rome, and then on to Athens, Kiev, Moscow, and St. Petersburg, where he met the czar. After that he visited Sweden, Copenhagen, Berlin, Prague, and Vienna before traveling to Paris, the final stop on his trip, where he had supper with Napoleon III.

While Douglas was journeying to all these exotic locations, I was traveling from Metamora to Bloomington to Mt. Pulaski on the circuit.

The Judge was rumored to be readying legislation for the organization of the Nebraska territory. The most important provision was popular sovereignty. As a Jacksonian Democrat, the Judge believed in letting the will of the people prevail. Through popular sovereignty, the people of a territory applying for statehood would vote to determine whether it would enter the union as a free or a slave state.

Why was Douglas proposing legislation that would overturn the Missouri Compromise of 1820, which had reduced the tension between the North and South over slavery?

Perhaps it was because he believed popular sovereignty was the answer to the continuing problem of slavery agitation. Perhaps it was because he wanted to extend the railroads west to the Pacific Ocean. Perhaps it was because he wanted the country to fulfill its destiny by expanding westward. Perhaps it was because he thought it was a horse he could ride to the presidency. Perhaps it was all of these.

It would mean that slavery could be extended into the territories, and I did not see how he could do it without repealing the Missouri Compromise. That was a line we could not permit him to cross.

Chapter 5

The Battleground Would Be the State of Illinois

On December 5, 1853, the first session of the 32nd Congress was called to order. Billy and I followed the proceedings through the newspapers and the *Congressional Globe*.

On a bitter winter morning a month later, I opened the office door into a room that was at least modestly warm. I removed my winter trappings, hung my coat on the peg, and sat down next to Billy.

"News from Washington?" I asked.

"Yes," he said, "but first tell me about Bobby."

"I think he's going to be fine. He hasn't shown any signs of hydrophobia. Wallace says he should be out of danger."

"Thank goodness. Do you think it was the madstone?"

"Billy, I don't think we rightly know. It may be that the dog didn't have it, but it may be that he did. It may be that the madstone cured him, and it may be that it didn't."

"Which do you think it is?"

"You know I always want to see the evidence, and in this case, I think there is some evidence the madstone worked. It's probably about the same with any medicine Wallace gives us."

"Do you want to hear about Douglas?"

"Maybe not now, I have an idea. The Newhall Family Singers have a concert tonight in the Senate Chamber. I heard them in Decatur when I was on the circuit last fall. It's their last one before the youngsters return to school, and you can meet my friend Mrs. Hillis. I talked to her after the performance, and she took a shine to me. If you come, we can have supper at the Cock and Crown, and you can tell me all about Douglas."

"I'm sure Mary will agree to that," said Billy. "Every so often she likes me out of the house so she can have supper with her mother."

In the early evening, we met at the Capitol. The singers were even better than their performance in Decatur. Billy was entranced, and after the concert he chatted amiably with Mrs. Hillis. I had to pry them apart and whisk him away for supper.

Although I didn't drink alcohol, I loved the scene at the Cock and Crown. We could feel the energy as we walked in. Everyone there was a friend or acquaintance, and through the smoke and raucous conversation, we greeted them as we walked to our favorite table.

"Billy," crowed James Haines, "I see you brought the old man with you tonight."

"No, Jim, the old man brought me!" Billy shot back.

Guffaws erupted and backs were slapped at all the surrounding tables.

As we sat down, the waiter pounded an enormous mug of beer down onto the table.

"It's the usual," said Billy quietly.

"No need to explain," I replied. "It's not the only contradiction in your life, friend Billy. One moment you're a temperance man and the next you're on a bender."

Billy mumbled something unintelligible, quaffed a large chug of his beer, and then said, "I see why you like that Lois Hillis."

"I do, but as my friend David Davis reminded me, I have taken my vows."

Billy paused, looked at me searchingly, and then said, "Lincoln, does it surprise you the women are sweet on you?"

It was an interesting observation, one that I could have brushed off, but I thought carefully about it and decided to reply.

"When I came to Springfield, all the rising men, including Judge Douglas, were dashing and at ease with the young women. I was neither, and I felt fortunate that Miss Todd paid some attention to me. She was the only one who believed there was more to me than my homely looks. I don't know that I've amounted to as much as she expected. After all, she could have married Douglas.

"So tell me," I continued, "what is Douglas doing now?"

"He has introduced legislation to organize the Nebraska territory."

"Which he did last year—and it failed," I responded. "He didn't get enough southern votes because he left the Missouri Compromise intact."

"And what is he doing this time to get more of them?"

"He's willing to repeal the Missouri Compromise, but he wants to do it without losing northern votes."

This was where Douglas was at his best, but this time he was on thinner ice. The issue was whether Congress would allow slavery to expand into the territories—the land in the Louisiana Purchase and the Mexican Cession from which more states could be created.

On three separate occasions, Congress had framed legislation on the issue. Under the Articles of Confederation, the Northwest Ordinance of 1787 prohibited slavery in the territory north of the Ohio River. In the Missouri

Compromise of 1820, states admitted north of a line extending west from the southern border of Missouri to the Rocky Mountains would be free, and states admitted south of that line would be slave. In the Compromise of 1850, states created from the Utah and New Mexico territory would choose to be free or slave through the process of popular sovereignty.

The heart of the issue was that Douglas claimed the policy of popular sovereignty established in the Compromise of 1850 took precedence over the Missouri Compromise and the Northwest Ordinance, allowing any newly admitted state to be slave or free.

As our conversation continued, I asked Billy, "So he wants popular sovereignly to take the place of the Missouri Compromise without actually repealing it?"

"That's it," responded Billy. "That way he thinks he can attract both northern and southern votes for his Nebraska bill."

I was angry. I raised my voice and pointed my finger in the air, and roared, "He is playing a dangerous game. If he succeeds in repealing the Missouri Compromise, he will overturn the law that has kept this country together for the past thirty years. He is the one who said, 'It is a sacred thing which no ruthless hand would ever be reckless enough to disturb.' It would be an abomination if he were able to persuade Congress to repeal it."

Billy countered, "He is the most powerful man in the Senate. He is a magician in crafting legislation."

"I know that," I said, "but surely you know what it would mean. If slavery expands into the territories there is no stopping it. Slavery could be reintroduced into states that are now free. Our only hope is to keep it contained to the South, which is what the Founders intended."

"How do you know that?" asked Billy.

"Look again at the Constitution. They outlawed the slave trade in 1808, and they never used the words slave or slavery. They didn't want to recognize it."

"And what did they think might happen?"

"That containing it would ultimately end it."

Billy looked at me with deep concern.

"Do you think that could actually happen?" he asked.

"I do, but we have to stop Douglas from the mischief he's up to with his notion of popular sovereignty."

Billy leaned back, took the last gulp of his beer, and ordered another.

I decided to change the subject.

"William, how is it that I have to hear you are running for mayor of Springfield from Billy the Barber?"

He looked at me with a puzzled expression.

"That was supposed to be a secret," he said sheepishly. "We wanted to surprise you. Did he tell you?"

"Heavens no! I know that Billy is very discreet. I pried it out of him."

"How did you do that?"

"William, that is what we lawyers do for a living."

"Do you think I will be elected?"

"You should, but if they believe you will go on one of your temperance tears again, I wouldn't be so sure."

The next day, I arrived at the office early. While Billy was engrossed in reading the newspapers, through the window I saw the sun rising in the east.

"Is there any news about Douglas?" I asked.

"He's making progress."

"What has he done about the Missouri Compromise?"

"The southern senators wanted a clearer statement of repeal. Douglas gave in and accepted an amendment from Senator Dixon, a Whig from Kentucky. He told Dixon, 'I will incorporate it in my bill though I know it will raise a hell of a storm.'"

Looking away from him, I contemplated this quietly. It would be more than a hell of a storm.

I turned back toward Billy and asked him, "Does his bill have a chance of passing?"

"Douglas knows how to work around any obstacle. He's done it before, and I think he may succeed this time as well. Repealing the Compromise will gain him the votes he needs. He even has the president onboard. They've also divided the territory into Kansas and Nebraska, which can become separate states."

"Are the anti-slavery men organizing?" I asked.

"The storm has come. The anti-slavery men in the House and Senate, led by Chase, Sumner, and Giddings, are organizing. They have published a broadside in the *National Era*."

"What does it say?"

"That the Nebraska bill is ' . . . a criminal betrayal of precious rights . . . that it will convert Kansas into a dreary region of despotism inhabited by masters and slaves . . . and the dearest interests of freedom and the Union are in imminent peril. . . .'"

"This is new, Billy," I said. "It is the language of the abolitionists. The extremes on both sides are pulling us apart."

"Lincoln," he replied, "it will be the most contentious congressional debate we've ever seen. They say the vote will come in six weeks. Douglas may have the votes this time."

"I hope not, Billy, I keep hoping he won't, but if he does, it will change everything."

He did get the votes. On March 4, 1854, after a five-and-a-half-hour speech by Douglas, by a vote of 37-14, the Senate passed the Kansas-Nebraska Act. On March 22, after acrimonious discussion, the House passed the bill by a vote of 113-100. On March 30, President Pierce signed the legislation into law.

Douglas had achieved his objective. In all likelihood, his motives were mixed. He had always believed in the expansion of the West. A transcontinental railroad was necessary to promote that goal. To achieve this, the Nebraska territory would have to be organized. What stood in the way was slavery. Douglas believed popular sovereignty was the answer, and he also believed the terrain of the western territory was hostile to slavery. He did not believe it would expand. If the Kansas-Nebraska Act succeeded, Douglas would be the favorite in the presidential election of 1856.

I was not convinced he grasped the possible consequences of the Kansas-Nebraska Act. He wanted desperately to craft legislation that would not alienate either the North or the South. On that point he had lost control of his coalition, and southern senators had forced him into an open repeal of the Missouri Compromise. I believed it was the Achilles heel in his legislation. I believed in containing slavery, and he risked its expansion to foster the country's destiny. He had crossed a line that had held for thirty years. I feared this would be "the fire bell in the night" that Jefferson had predicted in 1820.

The issue of slavery had always vexed me. All my life I had been an anti-slavery man, but the question was how to proceed in ending it—and how to do that without causing a war. I had witnessed it in the slave auctions in New Orleans and Lexington; I had thought about the slaves who served me at Speed's plantation and the Todd house; I had recalled the misery of the slaves on the steamboat with Speed; I had talked about slavery with Joshua Giddings and other friends, colleagues, and opponents; I had read about it in newspapers and in *Uncle Tom's Cabin*; I had pondered it on walks around Springfield and circuit buggy rides; and I had come to a conclusion: the negro was a human being and entitled to the rights established in the Declaration of Independence. Slavery was a moral wrong.

It was time for me to act on this belief.

I was now a different person from the man I was in 1849. I was tempered by political disappointment and defeat. The deaths of those close to me had caused me to find meaning and purpose in my continuing life. The compromises that made my marriage possible had taught me to accept the complexities of another person. From my law practice in Springfield and my days on the circuit, I had learned that human beings were flawed, and the lawyer's calling was to keep the peace. I had learned to live with my melancholy and to accept it as part of me, and that opening myself to my own sadness and the sadness of the world was a way to gain strength from it. My absence from politics had taught me the value of humility: to submerge my own desires into the cause of the greater good. I had become true to myself, and hence, I could be false to no man.

It was time for me to emerge from my political exile—to step out from the shadow of Douglas, and to step back into the political forum. I knew that the battleground would be the state of Illinois and that my antagonist would be Stephen Douglas.

Part Two

Chapter 6

Our Republican Robe Is Soiled

The scorching sun beat down on the prairie without mercy. For weeks there was no rain. Out on the prairie, the sun baked the coneflowers, the primroses, and the black-eyed Susans. They withered and turned brown. The birds fled to the deep forest, and there were no cheery calls in either the morning or the early evening. They were replaced with the grating choruses of locusts. The livestock preferred the slightly cooler shelter of the barns to grazing in the murderous sun, and horses balked at pulling their carriages. During the day, no rabbits darted through the parched prairie grass.

The time seemed out of joint.

Even so, I buried myself in the law library of the State Capitol. Billy took over most of our law cases—at least for a month. In the *Congressional Globe*, I read through the transcript of the Kansas-Nebraska debate, from January 4, when Douglas proposed it in the Senate, to March 17, when the Senate passed it, and ending with May 22, when the House followed suit.

I also researched the Missouri Compromise. My purpose was to prepare myself for the discussions and debates that I knew would reverberate around the country, but particularly in Illinois.

Often I was by myself, and when I was alone, I found my thoughts crystalizing on the political issues that threatened to tear the country apart. I was not sure when or in what forum I would be speaking about the Kansas-Nebraska Act and the repeal of the Missouri Compromise, but I wanted to be ready when that opportunity came. I wanted to introduce myself as an anti-slavery man and to speak out against its extension. I wanted to go to the heart of slavery and address it as a moral stain on the fabric of our democratic republic.

How could we adhere to the principles established in the Declaration of Independence while allowing slavery to exist in our country? I would advocate that we elect a Congress committed to reinstating the Missouri Compromise.

No sooner had I completed my research and drafted my response to the Kansas-Nebraska Act, than late one afternoon at home, ominous dark clouds gathered in the west. The sky continued to darken. A greenish tint emerged around the edges of the blackest clouds. As they swept overhead, a sharp wind cut across the street, creating spouts of dust and debris. Crisp flashes of lightning were followed by violent claps of thunder. Then came the punishing rain. Wave after wave ate the soil and carried it away into rivulets and gullies. A blinding bolt of lightning followed instantly by a frightening crack of thunder signaled the storm was directly overhead.

It did not relent. Throwing all its force into the battle, the wind intensified and rocked the walls of our sheltering house. I was not certain they would hold. I wondered how long the elderly oak across the street could withstand the elemental power of the wind. That tree had to be over a hundred years old. Could the huge roots of this ancient giant defy a primal force? They were locked in a titanic struggle. The upper branches bent in surrender, but, although they shook, the limbs seemed to be holding.

I felt a tug on my sleeve and looked around to see Bobby standing next to me. I was so immersed in the storm that I hadn't noticed him enter and cross the room.

"Papa, why are you looking out the window?" he asked.

I reached down, picked him up, and cradled him so that he could see out too.

"Why, Bobby, I'm watching to see if the oak tree can survive this terrible storm."

"It's very old, isn't it?" he inquired.

"Indeed it is—probably over a hundred years, maybe even older."

"Then hasn't it lived through storms like this?"

"I'm sure it has, probably many times."

At that moment, we noticed the tree starting to lean to one side. Sensing its advantage, the wind attacked furiously. Bobby cried out when the earth rose and fell away from a large, emerging root. Simultaneously, the trunk listed more dramatically, and more roots sprang from the ground.

The end came quickly. The weight of the falling trunk pushed down the limbs and branches. They cracked and groaned, and smashed to the ground with a final thump that shook the second floor of our house. The venerable tree lay on its side with its massive roots reaching upward to the sky. The wind howled victoriously, and the rain started to wash the dirt from the roots.

It happened so slowly and so quickly that we were both shocked.

Bobby asked, "Is it dead, Papa?"

"It's not dead yet, but we will have to saw it for firewood."

"Can't we put it back on its feet?"

"I'm afraid not, Bobby," I replied.

He buried his face into my shoulder and began to cry.

I did my best to comfort him.

If this was "the hell of a storm" that Stephen Douglas predicted, like our oak that had fallen, we might not survive.

The response to the Kansas-Nebraska Act was indicative of the sectional conflict that was now our political norm. In the South there was little reaction, but in the North, a growing chorus of voices was outraged. The Democrats were concerned about the 1854 and 1855 elections. In mid-August, when Douglas returned to Illinois after the congressional session had adjourned, he commented that he could follow a trail of light from Boston to Chicago from effigies of him that were burning.

He decided to campaign across Illinois in support of Democratic candidates. That would give him the opportunity to explain what he expected the Kansas-Nebraska Act to accomplish, and to bolster his political standing in the state.

At the same time I was dealing with a dilemma of my own. The passage of the Kansas-Nebraska Act had thrown the Illinois Whigs into confusion. We were thunderstruck and stunned, but we realized we must support each other.

My friend Richard Yates, an anti-Douglas Whig, was running for re-election in the 7th congressional district against the Democratic incumbent, Thomas Harris. He asked me to help him with his campaign, and I was delighted to accept. It meant I would be jumping back into politics. In my speeches in support of Yates, I would be able to attack Douglas and the Kansas-Nebraska Act. I was ready for this.

The Springfield Whigs urged me to run for the state legislature to increase support for Yates's candidacy. Not wanting to take a step backward, I refused. Defying my wishes when I was away, William Jayne, our family doctor, had Simeon Francis, the editor of the *Illinois Journal*, list Judge Logan and me as candidates for the legislature.

When Molly saw this, she flew over to Francis's office and demanded my name be removed.

On my return, Jayne visited me at our house and pressured me to run. I didn't know what to do. I was torn between my loyalty to my party and to my wife.

I paced up and down the parlor while Jayne was pressing me to let my name stand in the papers.

"No, I can't," I cried. "You don't know all. I say you don't begin to know half and that's enough."

Jayne did go to the paper and have my name reinstated.

I acceded and prevailed with Molly, protesting that I must support my party. I supposed my doing so would help Yates.

In late August, I began to give speeches on behalf of Yates's candidacy. In two appearances at Bloomington, I worked to refine my message.

Meanwhile, on September 1, Douglas encountered a hostile crowd when he spoke in Chicago. Northern Illinois was strongly anti-slavery, and he was heckled and interrupted so often that he stormed off the stage. His resolve deepened, and he began a statewide speaking tour.

On October 16, Douglas planned to speak in Peoria. Jesse Fell, a mutual friend, proposed that we debate the issues, but Douglas replied he would not share the platform with anyone. The best offer we could obtain was to speak in the late afternoon when Douglas finished. His strategy was that if the day were hot and humid and he had spoken for three hours, most of the crowd would not stay for another three hours of oratory.

When I had returned home from my term in Congress, I began to study Euclid's *Elements*. I wanted to understand Euclid's process of demonstrating his proofs, but I wanted to question his assertions rather than simply accepting them. I wanted to know how I might apply this understanding to my thinking, my writing, and my oral arguments.

As I continued to study Euclid, I was attracted to the beauty of his thinking. It was a model of logical, precise reasoning. When I couldn't sleep at home, I worked at the little desk in my bedroom with large heavy sheets of blank paper, a ruler, a compass, pencils, and ink in several colors.

I found my study of Euclid helpful as I constructed my arguments for the Peoria Speech. When I finished writing it, I committed it to memory and then rehearsed my delivery. After several weeks, I was ready for the encounter with Douglas in Peoria.

On the evening of October 15, I traveled from Pekin, where I'd been in court, to Peoria. I arrived at 2 a.m. and took a room at the Peoria House. The next morning my friends Abner Ellis, Elihu Powell, and Ben Irwin told me that Douglas had arrived the previous afternoon in a carriage pulled by four white horses. He was greeted by a welcoming committee, a corps of fife and drum, brass bands, cheers from a large crowd, and explosions from a cannon imported for the occasion. It was a suitable welcome for the great man of the age.

On my arrival, I was greeted by a grumpy old farmer who was the night clerk at the hotel.

The following morning, Ellis, Powell, and Irwin informed me that they had met with Douglas's cronies to make the final arrangements. We would be speaking from the portico of the courthouse, which was only eight years old and quite elegant. The weather would be sunny and temperate during the day and cool in the evening. Douglas would speak at 1 p.m. and I immediately after him. He would have an hour afterward to reply to me.

I had a brief encounter with Douglas in the hotel lobby just before lunch. He was sitting on a sofa reading copies of the *Peoria Republican* and the *Peoria Daily Union*.

He looked up and greeted me.

"Ah, my friend Lincoln, I hear you slipped into the hotel in the wee hours of the morning."

"Yes, Judge, my welcoming committee was the moon, the stars, and a solitary owl. I suspect there were some mice, but they were probably hiding from both the owl and Old Buck."

He threw his head back and said, "Let's dispense with the pleasantries. I know exactly why you are here, Lincoln. My friends were clucking about how we had a clear field, but I knew you'd show up."

"And why do you think I am here?"

"To claim we should never have repealed the Missouri Compromise, to prattle on about your cockamamie notion that our Founding Fathers were really anti-slavery men, and to continue your abolitionist rant about negro equality."

"Well, Judge, that's a tall order. You should stay and hear me today to see if I live up to your expectations."

"Pooh," he muttered and went back to reading the newspapers.

Slightly before one o'clock, Douglas climbed through a first-floor window in the courthouse onto the portico from which we would speak. From the portico, he could see locust trees blooming around the town square. Horses and mules pawed the ground in front of the hitching posts. Migrating geese honked overhead. Douglas was greeted with loud cheers from the huge crowd.

He was introduced by State Senator Washington Cockle, and then he began to speak. Douglas's address was a stirring rendition of all the arguments he'd made over the last several months for the Kansas-Nebraska Act and the repeal of the Missouri Compromise.

He said he was the chair of the Senate committee on territories when questions arose about organizing the Nebraska territory. In the Compromise of 1850, popular sovereignty was enacted into law to organize the Utah and New Mexico territories. Douglas believed the Compromise of 1850 had made the Missouri Compromise inoperative, and he agreed to repeal it. He proposed that popular sovereignty should apply to the Nebraska territory. This became law when the Kansas-Nebraska bill was passed by Congress and signed by President Pierce.

Popular sovereignty was the most basic right of our democratic republic: the right of self-government—the right of the people to decide whether their territory should become a slave or free state.

Slavery would not spread to states where the climate and terrain were unfit for it. His final argument was that the Kansas-Nebraska Act would end slavery agitation.

He spoke passionately and eloquently for the full three hours. If I'd been on the fence on these issues, he would have convinced me.

When he finished, the crowd began to call for me to speak.

I did not think this a good idea. They were tired and hungry, and, at best, their attention would wane. I called to them to go home, get something to eat, and return at 7 p.m. to hear me.

It was already dark when we returned at seven o'clock. Like Douglas, I climbed onto the speakers' platform through the portico window. While he was short and stubby, I was long and lanky, and my entry was more awkward. When I looked out, I could see that the crowd, lit by the candles in the lampposts and windows of the neighboring houses, was larger than the one Douglas had addressed earlier.

I was introduced, and it was time to begin.

I opened by stating my topic would be the repeal of the Missouri Compromise and the case for restoring it.

I then followed with a simple, but important, point.

"I wish to say that I do not propose to question the patriotism, or to assail the motives of any man or class of men; but rather to strictly confine myself to the naked merits of the question."

Next came a short history of how the country had dealt with slavery extension prior to the Kansas-Nebraska Act, through the Northwest Ordinance, the Missouri Compromise, and the Compromise of 1850. I restated my conviction that the Founding Fathers had opposed the extension of slavery, and set it on a course toward extinction.

"The foregoing history may not be precisely accurate in every particular; but I am sure it is sufficiently so, for all the uses I shall attempt to make of it, and in it, we have before us, the chief material enabling us to correctly judge whether the repeal of the Missouri Compromise is right or wrong.

"I think, and shall try to show, that it is wrong; wrong in its direct effect, letting slavery into Kansas and Nebraska–and wrong in its prospective principle, allowing it to spread to every other part of the wide world, where men can be found inclined to take it."

I declared that although I had come to hate slavery as a monstrous injustice, a stain on the fabric of our democratic republic, I had no prejudice against the Southern people.

"They are just what we would be in their situation. If slavery did not now exist amongst them, they would not introduce it. If it did now exist amongst us, we should not instantly give it up. When Southern people tell us they are no more responsible for the origin of slavery than we; I acknowledge the fact. When it is said that the institution exists; and that it is very difficult to get rid of, in any satisfactory way, I can understand and appreciate the saying. I surely will not blame them for not doing what I should not know how to do myself."

I turned to the principle of self-government on which Douglas made his case for popular sovereignty. I had to counter his argument that the Missouri Compromise violated the sacred right of self government.

"The doctrine of self government is right–absolutely and eternally right–but it has no just application, as here attempted.

Or perhaps I should rather say that whether it has such just application depends upon whether a negro is not or is a man. If he is not a man, why in that case, he who is a man may, as a matter of self-government, do just as he pleases with him. But if the negro is a man, is it not to that extent, a total destruction of self-government, to say that he too shall not govern himself? When the white man governs himself that is self-government; but when he governs another man, that is more than self-government–that is despotism. If the negro is a man, why then my ancient faith teaches me "that all men are created equal;" and there can be no moral right in connection with one man's making a slave of another.

"No man is good enough to govern another man, without the other's consent. I say this is the leading principle–the sheet anchor of American republicanism. Now the relations of masters and slaves is a total violation of this principle.

"I have done with this mighty argument of self government. Go, sacred thing! Go in peace."

After many years, much experience, and deep reflection, I had finally come to the conclusion that the negro was human and that he was entitled to the basic human rights established in the Declaration of Independence.

"Equal justice to the South, it is said, requires us to consent to the extending of slavery to the territories. That is to say, inasmuch as you do not object to my taking my hog to Nebraska, therefore I must not object to you taking your slave. Now, I admit this is perfectly logical, if there is no difference between hogs and negroes.

"Senator Douglas has always said that this government was made for white people and not for the negroes. In this remark of the Judge, there is a significance which I think is the key to the great mistake he has made in this Nebraska measure. It shows the

Judge has no very vivid impression that the negro is a human; and consequently has no idea that there can be any moral questioning legislating about him.

"Slavery is founded in the selfishness of man's nature– opposition to it, is in his love of justice. These principles are an eternal antagonism; and when brought into collision so fiercely, as slavery expansion brings them, shocks, and throes, and convulsions must ceaselessly follow."

As I came toward the end, I felt it necessary to warn about the conflict I foresaw for Kansas with Douglas's principle of popular sovereignty.

"Some Yankees, in the East, are sending emigrants to Nebraska, to exclude slavery from it; and, so far as I can judge, they expect the question to be decided by voting, in some way or other. But the Missourians are awake too. They are within a stone's throw of the contested ground. They hold meetings, and pass resolutions, in which not the slightest allusion to voting is made. They resolve that slavery already exists in the territory; that more shall go there; that they, remaining in Missouri will protect it; and that abolitionists shall be hung, or driven away. Through all this, bowie-knives and six-shooters are seen plainly enough; but never a glimpse of the ballot box. And, really, what is to be the result of this? Each party WITHIN, having numerous and determined backers WITHOUT, is it not probable that the contest will come to blows, and bloodshed? Could there be a more apt invention to bring about collision and violence, on the slavery question, than this Nebraska project is?"

I made a final plea for the restoration of the Missouri Compromise.

"The Missouri Compromise ought to be restored. For the sake of the Union, it ought to be restored. We ought to elect a House of Representatives which will vote its restoration.

"Fellow countrymen–Americans south, as well as north, slavery is undermining and fatally violating the noblest political system the world has ever seen. This is not the taunt of enemies, but the warning of friends.

"Our republican robe is soiled, and trailed in the dust. Let us re-purify it. Let us turn and wash it white, in the spirit, if not the blood, of the Revolution. Let us re-adopt the Declaration of Independence, and with it, the practices, and policy, which harmonize with it. Let North and South–let all Americans–let all lovers of liberty everywhere–join in the great and good work. If we do this, we shall not only have saved the Union; but we shall have so saved it, as to make it, and keep it, forever worthy of the saving. We shall have saved it, that the succeeding millions of free happy people, the world over, shall rise up, and call us blessed, to the latest generations."

During much of my speech, the crowd was silent, in some parts deathly silent. At the end, however, they erupted into loud "Huzzahs!" and waved white handkerchiefs energetically in the cool night air. When I raised my arms in response, I was treated to more cheers and applause.

The outpouring of support continued for several minutes and was deeply gratifying. It gave me the confidence that I had spoken for this huge gathering of people as well as for myself.

After the speech, I realized it marked a change in me. I spent several months preparing it. The research was extensive. In choosing the examples to make a logical argument, I relied on my training and experience as a lawyer. It was like making a closing argument to a jury.

New for me was allowing the structure and rhythm of the language to help me find my voice. Writing the speech, I struggled to make sure each word was right, but before long I felt the power of the words sweeping through me and flowing from me. Somehow the words and phrases and sentences fit together and became the form through which the meaning emerged.

Where did those words come from? I could not be certain, but I believed they were coming from the reading I'd done all my life. Since Eddie's death, I had regularly read the Bible that Speed's mother had given me when I stayed for six weeks at Farmington in the summer of 1841. I'd read most of Shakespeare's plays, many of them two or three times. I was not trying to imitate what I'd read. The rhythms were now deep inside me.

Delivering the speech also felt different.

The political message was clear. I conceded we had to accept slavery in the states where it existed. This was the compromise the Founders accepted. But they were against extending it. We could not allow that to happen. The Kansas-Nebraska Act opened the door to the extension of slavery.

The moral message stirred a passion I felt for our democracy—particularly the principles of the Declaration of Independence—and for the plight of the negro. The negro was a man, a human being, with the natural rights promised to all Americans. In speaking of this, I let myself be carried by a force both within and beyond me. It was like a horse striding effortlessly into a full gallop. My physical presence dissolved, and I felt a connection with the audience through which energy passed from me to them and then back to me.

I was alive with purpose as I had never been before.

Chapter 7

No Longer Friends

I was resting on the sofa in our office with the *Illinois State Register* over my face, when I heard the door open, and Billy Herndon walked into the room.

"Good morning, Lincoln," he chirped brightly. "What does the world look like from under there?"

"Flat, very flat," I said lugubriously.

He walked over to the sofa and sat down on the worn cushion near my feet. I could feel him plop down.

"Well, I hope you cheer up by this afternoon," he said. "David Davis is coming to see us. He's staying in Springfield until you set off for Pekin in the first week of November."

I pulled the paper from my face and propped my head up on the sofa arm so that I could see Billy. His face always shone with eagerness and vitality, although I could see a wisp of concern.

"Ah," I said, "thank you for reminding me. I am looking forward to being on the circuit again."

"How long will you be gone this time?"

"Because of the elections, a little less than six weeks."

"I don't know what you like about it," he said with a hint of disdain in his voice. "You trek five hundred miles through the wilderness of central Illinois; you stop at thirteen county seats for a few days or at most a week in each of those flea-bitten towns; the cases are about stolen pigs or who is responsible for sheep rot; you stay in dilapidated inns and taverns, eight men sleeping together in one room with two each in a bed, bedbugs and mosquitoes feasting on you all night long; the food is miserable; you have two or three cases a day with little or no time to prepare; and the courtroom proceedings are sometimes interrupted by drunks. How could anyone enjoy that for more than a week or two?"

"Billy, don't forget that it helps to pay the bills."

He looked perplexed and said, "Just a few cases like the ones we're getting now would pay as much, if not more."

"Ah, my young friend, you have never seen the charm of it.

"In those small towns, which you disparage unfairly, you see everyday life. On the circuit I have seen every form of human depravity, and yet I still believe in mankind.

"Yes, the cases come at you quickly, but they are always interesting because there is such variety, and you have to be agile and quick on your feet.

"The food is tolerable if you don't look at it too closely.

"The sleeping quarters suffice if you can put up with Davis, Lamon, and Swett, who snore like locomotives.

"And Billy, the camaraderie is second to none. We eat together, we sleep together, we try cases together and sometimes against each other, we entertain each other at the tavern firesides by night. I get to tell them the story of the exploding dog and to recite "The Raven," and sometimes we import entertainers who are circulating through the towns and villages just as we do.

"I have you to manage our practice, and I am free to live life on the open road.

"Billy, there's nothing like it!"

Later that afternoon, we were disturbed by a knock on the door. Billy opened it, and a portly, well-dressed gentleman entered and bellowed, "Messrs. Lincoln and Herndon hard at work, I dare say."

"Davis," we said simultaneously.

David Davis was a large man; everything about him was large: his frame was large and corpulent, his head was large, his mind was expansive, and his heart knew no boundary.

Our friendship began when he was elected the judge of the Illinois Eighth Judicial Circuit in 1848. We were together twice a year for three months when we rode the circuit. After a rigorous day, in the evening hours, we relaxed in his room, telling stories about politics, the law, and our early experiences.

Billy began lightheartedly, "I presume you have come to collect the senior partner to bring justice to the people of central Illinois."

Davis, who enjoyed verbal banter, replied, "Yes, like Don Quixote, I am here to request the services of Sancho Panza."

"Friend Davis," I replied, "I am flattered by the allusion, but as I recall, Don Quixote was tall and thin, and Sancho was short and fat. The knight errant sought to change the world, but his squire was more dubious. One was impulsive and the other more passive."

Addressing me, Billy jumped in, "So which is Davis and which is you?"

"Good question!" I admonished them.

"And the answer is?" asked Davis.

"Infinitely complex," I replied. "It may well be that one can't exist without the other—which is to say that each is part of the other and the other is part of each."

"So saith our backwoods sage," said Davis, having the last word as usual.

At this point came another knock on the door.

"Ah, it's probably Swett. I invited him to join us."

"Well done, I always enjoy his company," I responded.

As Davis opened the door, a tall young man entered and shook hands with him. They were close friends, in part because they were both from Bloomington.

Leonard Swett was sixteen years younger than I. Tall and handsome, he grew up in Maine, attended Colby College, studied law, and then volunteered to fight in the Mexican War. After the war, he settled in Clinton, a town south of Bloomington, where he became a school teacher and practiced law. He became my friend by traveling the circuit with the rest of us.

Although he enjoyed the company of the circuit lawyers, there was something removed and distant in Swett. For me, this made him all the more intriguing. Once we became friends our bond deepened.

Davis and Swett seated themselves on the sofa, while Billy and I drew up chairs, creating a small circle.

"Lincoln," began Davis, "your Peoria speech has made a splash in the Whig newspapers. They're saying they never expected anything like it from you."

Everyone was silent for a moment, and then I replied, "Well, I'm glad to have exceeded their expectations."

Again there was silence, which was broken when Billy observed, "It was the profoundest speech you have made in your whole life. Even the *Register* has grudgingly admitted it was 'an oratorical gem,' although they don't agree with any of it. And listen to this editorial from the *Peoria Republican*, 'It was a truly able and masterly speech. We have never heard the subjects treated with such eloquence, nor have we often seen a speaker acquit himself with greater apparent ease and self-possession.'"

Swett looked at me earnestly and added, "We've all heard you on the stump before, Lincoln, and it was different."

I got up from my chair, stretched out to my full height, walked over to the green-covered table, and paused for a moment to think.

Then I looked back over at them and said, "Of course it was different, my friends, of course it was different. Everything is different. Everything is changing. Douglas had no idea his plan would increase slavery agitation, and the political parties are collapsing—all of this with consequences no one has foreseen."

I quickly realized I had injected a serious tone into a relaxed gathering. I sat down in my chair and tried to lighten the mood by asking, "What should we do next?"

Billy followed up by asking, "Well, I suppose we should try to figure out what Douglas will do next?"

Davis patted his stomach as if sending a message that he was hungry, but then said, "As far as we know, he has come back to Illinois with his tail between his legs. Instead of being a conquering hero, he's encountered a stinging rebuke to his Kansas-Nebraska Act. To his utmost surprise, they ate him alive in Chicago. I believe his plan is to travel around the state giving hopelessly long speeches defending his ill-conceived plan for expanding slavery."

"But what should we do?" followed up Billy.

There was another long silence.

Finally Davis spoke again, "I expect he got another unpleasant surprise when our friend Lincoln skewered him in

Peoria. I'd suggest that Lincoln follow him to each town and give the same rejoinder we heard the other night. Douglas will quail before anything so logical and convincing."

"What if Douglas won't debate?" asked Swett.

"He probably will try to speak late in the afternoon and then skip town," answered Billy.

"My guess is that he'll duck Lincoln one way or another," said Davis. "The word in his camp is that Lincoln has proven a more formidable adversary than they expected."

"How do you know?" I asked.

He smiled and winked at me, "I have my ways!"

"Someone close to him?" I followed up.

He gave me an inscrutable look, and then said, "I believe someone representing Douglas will be here in a matter of minutes."

We all looked at him in amazement. Davis was highly respected for knowing and applying the law. He was also known for his devotion to the law. He had ruled against me as often as he ruled for me. Although he was above all a judge, David Davis was also fascinated with politics. He had an intuitive sense of them that rivaled anyone else's. Our Whig principles also drew us closer together, and on the circuit, we talked about political trends and subtleties late into the night.

Davis changed the focus and direction of our conversation. "What is happening to our political parties?" he asked.

This brought a prolonged silence. No one ventured an explanation or a theory. It was complex, and I was the only one willing to try.

"At the moment the Whigs are in the most serious trouble. The slavery issue split the northern and southern Whigs, and we were badly divided in 1852. The Free Soil Party started it. They pulled anti-slavery men out of both parties, and while the Democrats returned to their fold, many Whigs have not. Somehow the Democrats have been able to hold the different wings of their party together."

"It could be that Jefferson and Jackson, who were both southerners, were just as popular in the north," Billy observed.

"And they were winners," added Davis. "That always counts in politics. Since Jackson, they've won every election but for Harrison and Taylor."

"Somehow we seem to do better when we run a general," said Swett, "except for 'Old Fuss and Feathers!'"

"And our hero Clay lost three times," I said mournfully.

Getting back to the Democrats, Billy, who also had a mind for politics, continued the conversation by saying, "The Democrats have their hands full with the Know Nothings."

"Those ghastly nativists," responded Davis. "I've never quite understood how they can hate the immigrants and the Catholics yet still be anti-slavery in principle."

At this point I rose from my chair, raised my voice, and declared, "As a nation, we began by declaring that 'all men are created equal.' We now practically read it 'all men are created equal, except negroes.' When the Know Nothings get control, it will read, 'all men are created equal, except negroes, and foreigners, and Catholics.' When it comes to this I should prefer emigrating to some country where they make no pretense of loving liberty—to Russia, for instance!"

There was a loud rapping on the door.

We were all mystified, but Swett walked over to the door and opened it.

A well-dressed gentleman entered the office without looking at anyone in particular. None of us knew who he was.

"Is the Honorable Abraham Lincoln present this afternoon?" he asked.

"Indeed he is," answered Davis imperiously.

"Which of you gentlemen is the Honorable Mr. Lincoln?"

"I am," I replied.

He eased closer toward me and removed an envelope from his inner coat pocket.

"Mr. Lincoln, I am here representing Senator Douglas. The Senator requests that you meet with him tomorrow afternoon at 2:30 p.m. in his suite at the American Hotel."

He presented me the letter.

"The senator also requests the favor of an immediate reply."

I opened the letter, read it, and said, "Tell him I will be there tomorrow."

"Thank you, Mr. Lincoln. I will inform the senator," said the unknown gentleman. He turned away from us and retreated through the door and down the steps.

A brief silence descended on us, but finally Swett asked, "What was that all about?"

Davis responded, "I don't know, but we will find out tomorrow." He gave me a wink as he and the others rose from their chairs to leave.

As I walked home, I wondered why Douglas would want to see me.

Surely this was not just a social visit. He and I had known each other for twenty years, and, although we had been friends, we hadn't seen much of each other since he was elected to the Senate in 1847. Our meetings were always cordial, and there were a number of political issues upon which we agreed, but our fundamental difference on the slavery issue caused friction between us.

I admired his political skills, and his national success eclipsed my achievements, but I sensed he shifted his positions for political or personal gain. I was surprised that he defended the Missouri Compromise so strongly in 1849 and was willing to repeal it five years later. I was known as trimmer, someone who could modify his views on an issue, but not someone who reversed positions. I was not sure I could trust the Judge. Politicians from opposing parties could be friends, but the friendship was based on respect for the other person's integrity.

The following afternoon, I walked the short distance to the American House on the corner of Sixth and Adams Streets. It was, of course, the best hotel in town, and Douglas was staying in the best suite the hotel had to offer. I climbed the stairs and knocked on his door.

It opened, and standing just behind it was Senator Stephen A. Douglas. I was puzzled to find him somewhat disheveled. He had not shaved, his hair was not combed, and there was a hint of red in his cyes. His shirt was lightly wrinkled, and his pants hung down over his shoes.

He greeted me warmly and escorted me to an elegant room he was using for private meetings. We sat down in the maroon leather armchairs for our discussion.

Douglas stood up and moved to the sideboard on which sat decanters of sherry, brandy, and whiskey.

He poured himself a glass of whiskey, and then said, "Come, Lincoln, have a drink with me." His voice was noticeably hoarse.

"No, thank you, Judge," I replied.

"What's the problem. Do you belong to a temperance society?"

"No, but I am temperate in that I don't drink anything."

He placed the glass on the table to the side of his chair and lit a cigar. Smoke billowed out into the room.

He locked his eyes on mine and asked the first question.

"Lincoln, why are you running for the state legislature? You were done with that in 1842. Is that the only place you can win an election?"

I held my eyes steadily on his.

"You know the reason. I ran to support Yates."

"I surmised that, but how can you take such a backward step?"

"A Whig does what he can to support his party."

"Ah, walking the plank for each other. Don't you realize you are committing political suicide, or is there more to this? If enough anti-slavery men are elected to the legislature, are you thinking of challenging Shields for the Senate seat?"

"That had occurred to me."

"But if you are a member of the legislature, you can't run for the Senate."

"I could resign my seat in the legislature."

"You could do that, but it would be another blunder. The voters will feel deceived and never vote for you again."

I ignored this and looked away.

He tried another line of attack.

"Lincoln, how could you run for the Senate when your party is in tatters? The vote will be splintered, and you will never gain a majority."

I replied, "The slavery issue is splitting my party, but it is nothing compared to what the Kansas-Nebraska Act will do to your party. My goal may be the Senate, but yours is the presidency. You have thrown it away with the fiasco that will come of Kansas-Nebraska."

He gave me a look of utter disdain and yelled, "Lincoln, do you know who I am? I will not stand for insults from a political nobody."

I refocused, sat forward in my chair, and asked him, "Judge, why have you invited me here today?"

The muscles in his face tightened, and his mouth twisted into a scowl. He took a gulp of whiskey, pointed his finger at me, and shouted, "Lincoln, I want to know why you are following me from place to place in this state, slandering me and making false statements about my record."

"Judge," I said, "the only thing that separates us and motivates me is your unwillingness to see the negro as a man and your contempt for him."

He sat back in his chair and looked at me with a quizzical expression. He seemed perplexed.

"Why is there disagreement between us on this subject? What is the nigger to either you or me? You say he will never have political or social equality with the white race. In fact, you want to send him back to Africa. What happens if they don't want to go?"

"Judge, no one has an answer for what happens if the slaves are freed. Our disagreement is on the extension of slavery. That's what the Kansas-Nebraska Act allows. If we restore the Missouri Compromise, slavery will be contained and eventually die."

"But, Lincoln, we've already been through this. Slavery will never expand into the territories because the climate and geography are hostile. The settlers will vote to exclude slavery. Popular sovereignty is the answer to the slavery issue. You will see."

There was no need to repeat the arguments we'd had publicly about these issues. The tension in the room seemed to ease.

His manner turned friendly and he appeared to relax.

"Lincoln, let's look at it another way. We can work together.

"We are both western men. You came here from Kentucky, and I from Vermont. We have made lives for ourselves in the West.

"You're a railroad man, and so am I. We both know the railroads are the key to westward expansion, and that by expanding west our country will fulfill its destiny. Why, if it weren't for your wife, you would have been the governor of the Oregon territory! Work with me and not against me, and we'll accomplish all these things together."

"A pretty picture, Judge, but for one flaw."

"What's that?"

"What to do about slavery."

"Lincoln, you can help me shut down slavery agitation. Once that's done, we can turn to our real business—crossing this continent and becoming the greatest country in the world."

"And you would have a westward expansion presidency?"

"Yes, Lincoln, that's my goal."

His vision was powerful and seductive, but the lives of four million people, descendants from people brought to America against their will, were nothing to him. As he often said, he didn't give a damn about them.

"Just remember, Judge, your colleague Seward has said that anyone who spells the word negro with two g's will never be elected president."

"That damned abolitionist," he muttered.

He could sense that I didn't have the slightest interest in his offer, and he decided to try one last ploy.

"Come, Lincoln, I can help you grow rich. I've bought land along the northern route of the railroad from Chicago to the coast. I'll slip you the map with the St. Louis route."

"Judge, we go back a long way, but I've chosen a different direction from you. As you know, I cannot ignore the negro's plight. I cannot condemn him to an institution that destroys his soul, and because he is a man, he has a soul."

"If you continue with this nonsense, I will tar you as an abolitionist, and you will be finished in politics. Somehow you've crawled out of your hole, but this time you'll never be heard from again."

"Well, Judge, on that note, we should part."

He got up from his chair, stubbed out his cigar, and ignoring me, walked toward the door.

It appeared to me that he was trying to control his anger. He was breathing deeply.

As I moved to the door myself, he raised his arm in a gesture that I believed was preliminary to shaking my hand. Instead he held up his forearm to bar me from leaving.

I could tell this was not an aggressive gesture, but simply that he wished me to stay for a minute.

"Lincoln," he said, "as I'm sure you've noticed, I am very hoarse. I am going to call off my events in Lacon and Princeton. I'd request that you do the same."

"Right, Judge, if that is your intent, then I will do the same."

He smiled at me, we shook hands, and as I left, I felt a tinge of sadness that we were parting as adversaries and no longer friends.

Chapter 8

The Crowning Achievement of My Life

As a politician, I had a goal that would be the crowning achievement of my life. In all likelihood it would be a goal I would never achieve, but it represented the office to which I aspired. My aspiration was to serve the state of Illinois in the United States Senate.

Normally one might serve several terms in the House of Representatives, and then be considered by his party as a contender for a Senate seat. It was highly competitive just to be in contention. A further complication was that, while the winner of most other elections was decided by popular vote, a senator was elected by the state legislators. The determining factor was which party had a majority of the state representatives and state senators.

When I was not renominated for the House, my opportunity to be a U.S. senator evaporated. There were exceptions, and my path in politics was never straight, but the likelihood of achieving my dream was minimal.

What changed this was my Peoria speech. The full text was published in the *Illinois Daily Journal*, the Whig newspaper in Springfield. It gained attention around the state. I became known as a leader in the anti-slavery movement in Illinois, but unfortunately this came at a time when the political parties were in chaos in Illinois and across the nation. I wanted to remain a Whig, but the situation was so fluid that no one knew what would happen.

David Davis, Leonard Swett, and Billy Herndon became my informal advisors. They were anti-slavery Whigs as well and had a personal interest in our discussions. We met monthly, in Bloomington or Springfield, to review the recent political developments and to develop a strategy for proceeding.

Shortly after the November elections of 1854, we met in the Lincoln and Herndon law office to discuss the meaning of the state and national contests. Our meetings were not so serious that we couldn't indulge in some light-hearted banter.

"Billy," said Swett, "has Lincoln told you about the time I first met him?"

Billy replied he had not.

Davis and I looked slightly uncomfortable.

As Swett began, our faces colored and our embarrassment was obvious to the others.

"That fall, I joined the circuit in Danville. When I called at the hotel it was after dark, and I was told Lincoln was upstairs in Davis's room. I knocked on the door, and two voices, almost simultaneously, yelled, 'Come in.'

"You can imagine my astonishment when I entered and found two men, dressed for bed, engaging in a lively pillow fight. Davis was puffing like a lizard, and Lincoln was flailing with his arms as if he were a windmill.

"Once I was safely inside, they resumed it.

"Davis gave Lincoln a hefty whack on the back and was about to deliver another blow to his head, when Lincoln ducked, grabbed Davis's pillow, and slugged him in the gut. Blow after blow was struck with a slight advantage for Lincoln because there was so much of Davis. When they exhausted themselves, they turned toward me and grinned.

"I looked at them in utter disbelief, but finally stammered, 'What are you two doing? I would never . . . '

'Never what?' asked Davis.

'Never have thought you would do anything like that.'

'For heavens sake, Swett, stop being such a stick-in-the-mud and join us,' Davis said, tossing me a pillow."

When Swett ended his story, Billy was so nonplussed he didn't know what to say.

I took up the slack and moved us to the purpose of our meeting.

"The results of the state and national elections are encouraging," I began. "The Democrats have sustained major losses nationally and also in our state legislature. Kansas-Nebraska has been a millstone around their necks."

Davis continued, "We have a small majority of anti-Nebraska men in the legislature."

Turning to me, Swett observed, "Lincoln, that opens up a door for you to run for the Senate if you are interested."

Was I interested? Eight years had passed since I had run for elective office, and not being renominated for Congress in 1848 still hurt, but the fire of ambition continued to burn inside me. I was interested.

"I am," I said.

"Your wife will be pleased to hear that!" exclaimed Billy.

"You stand a good chance," said Davis. "We must organize on your behalf, but the first thing you must do is resign from the legislature."

"Douglas told me about that in October. I hadn't realized it."

Billy warned, "You have to do it, but it will be seen as self-serving. It will give Douglas the good fortune to deflect that issue from himself and onto you."

"There's nothing we can do about that," said Davis. "We'll just have to paint it a little thicker on him."

"We have to move fast because the vote is in early February," added Swett. "Shields is Douglas's man running for re-election, but the Democrats do not have a majority. Trumbull may enter as the candidate of the anti-Nebraska Democrats, but those votes are up for grabs. On our side we'll have the Whigs, but we have to get as many of those anti-Nebraska Democrats as we can, especially the Free-Soilers."

"What about the Know Nothings?" asked Billy.

"I don't think we should write them off," I replied. "Although we find their beliefs repellent, they might be with us because they are against slavery expansion. Every vote will count."

"Our problem will be with the northern men of the state," said Davis. "They are closer to abolition than we are." Looking over at me, he continued, "They are still angry at you for removing yourself from the central committee of the Illinois Republican Party. We'll have to convince them you can be trusted."

I added, "I'd estimate at this point there are 44 Whigs and anti-Nebraska Democrats in the assembly and 13 in the Senate; the Democrats have 31 in the assembly and 12 in the Senate. We have the problem of persuading the Democrats to vote for a Whig. We'll also have to keep those anti-Nebraska Democrats with us and win on an early ballot. Some may slip away from us if the balloting goes on too long."

Davis pushed us forward with a plan.

"Lincoln, you have friends all over the state. You must write as many of them as you can—political friends, friends from the circuit, newspaper editors, business leaders, and some of the legislators. You should also write Elihu Washburne. He's very powerful, and might even bring Joshua Giddings to Chicago to speak for you. I will write letters to everyone I know, and Swett has offered to travel the state twisting the arms of his friends and acquaintances. He has also agreed to write letters. Billy, you will be useful with the abolitionists in the north. They believe you are leaning toward abolition, and they are hopeful you can convert your partner. We want to come to the vote in February with Lincoln as the leading contender. Things are moving quickly, and we should meet again in two weeks."

We parted, each of us with his assignment from Davis. I was encouraged by his optimism. I did have friends whom I'd known from our days on the circuit, and many of them were active in politics. I was ready to run with renewed vigor.

That night I sat with Molly by the fireplace. Bright flames emerged from the crackling logs, and we were sitting opposite each other in our comfortable chairs.

"You must work feverishly this time," said Molly. "We've seen opportunities slip between your fingers before."

"I have always wanted this one. I will not hold back. We are so close, and Davis thinks there's a good chance we will win."

"Just remember how you have misjudged your opponents in the past. Take nothing for granted, and let no one take advantage of your good nature."

"I have to mask my 'lean and hungry look,' but it will be there, I assure you."

"What does Davis think we should do now?"

"I am to write my friends and everyone who is undecided—even some who are leaning against me."

She did not speak for a few moments. Then with a look of determination, she spoke sharply, "Davis is right. We must marshal all our friends, persuade the undecided, and keep watch on our enemies."

"My dear, they are not our enemies. They may oppose me for my position on slavery; some say I am not radical enough and others say I have gone too far. They are my opponents, but not my enemies."

"I sometimes fear you do not have the fire inside you to win in politics."

"It is there, Molly, but I prefer to mask it."

"Be careful the mask does not fit too well."

Shc paused and then asked, "To whom are you to write?"

"To Elihu Washburne, Zebina Eastman, Owen Lovejoy, Abraham Smith, Charles Henry Ray, and Jesse Norton, at least to start."

"Don't forget Charles Hoyt, for whom you won that patent case, Jonathan Scammon in Chicago, Jacob Harding of Paris, Thomas Henderson of Toulon, and Joseph Gillespie with whom you jumped out of the window to prevent a quorum in the legislature."

"Yes, my dear, they are all on the list."

I leaned down and picked up the newspaper, but Molly continued, "I learned from Julia Trumbull this morning that Douglas spoke in Princeton last night."

"What?" I cried.

"Yes, his voice was hoarse, but he spoke to a huge crowd for two hours. He was happy to joust with you in absentia."

"What a scoundrel!" I cried again. "I made a horrible mistake to take him at his word."

"My dear, Mr. Lincoln, once again you are too trusting."

"How sad," I said. "I was hoping, through all this political strife, we might keep a thread of friendship, but I now see that is impossible."

"He has one thing in mind, and that is to destroy you."

She was right. I was hoping that a thread of friendship could still exist between Douglas and me, and I was loath to see it cut. Ambition could destroy friendships, but with purpose reawakened, I was ready to let my ambition carry me forward.

Late that night I sat at the little desk in my bedroom and wrote the first of my letters for the Senate campaign.

Mr. Charles Hoyt

Dear Sir:

You used to express a good deal of partiality for me; and if you are still so, now is the time. Some friends here are really for me, for the U.S. Senate; and I should be very grateful if you could make a mark for me from among your members. Please write me at all events, giving me the names, post-offices, and "political position" of members round about you. Direct to Springfield.

Yours truly

A. LINCOLN—

T. J. Henderson, Esq

My dear Sir—

It has come round that a Whig may, by possibility, be elected to the U.S. Senate; and I want the chance of being the man. You are a member of the Legislature, and have a vote to give. Think it over, and see whether you can do better than to go for me.

Yours truly

A. LINCOLN—

After finishing several more letters, I blew out the candle, and, since I was already wearing my nightshirt, I retired to my bed.

The following morning, my friends and I met in my law office. Billy and I should have travelled to Bloomington, but Davis decided that he and Swett would come to Springfield to hear the latest news about the upcoming election.

We met around the table. Even though we knew company was coming, Billy and I had not picked up the office. Although it looked higgledy-piggledy, Billy and I generally knew where everything was. We did have a pile under my hat that was marked, "If you can't find it, look here."

Davis, who was our de facto leader, called the meeting to order.

"Lincoln, have you written your letters?"

"I have," I replied.

"And you, Swett?"

Swett nodded that he had.

"Has anyone encountered opposition?" asked Davis.

There was silence for a moment, and then Swett offered a disconcerting piece of news.

"Abraham Smith," he reported, "is a holdout because Lincoln won a libel case against him. Smith also hasn't forgiven Lincoln for representing Matson, who was trying to recover his slaves."

"Some of the anti-Nebraska Democrats in Springfield are still angry at Lincoln for resigning from the legislature," added Billy. "It's embarrassing that a Democrat won Lincoln's seat in the special election. Shields said it was 'the best Christmas joke of the season!'"

"I'm concerned about something I heard last night," said Swett. "If Shields begins to fade, the Democrats may try to rally behind Governor Matteson. He's been able to straddle the pro-Nebraska and the anti-Nebraska Democrats. If he gets Shields's votes and then picks up a few anti-Nebraska men because they won't vote for a Whig, he could win."

"Well, bothersome as those reports are," scowled Davis, "they are outweighed by some very good news. Washburne is doing his damnedest to help Lincoln win. He has lined up Eastman for us, and he's gotten Giddings to buttonhole Lovejoy. Washburne writes that Giddings 'would walk clear to Illinois to elect you.'"

Davis paused to clear his throat and then continued, "Even more important is that Washburne has Charles Henry Ray aboard. He's very influential. He wrote Washburne, 'I do desire to lend a helping hand to checkmate the rascals who are making our government the convenient tool of the slave power; and if I can best do so by going for Lincoln, why, I am on hand.'"

Davis continued, "I'm also delighted to let you know that Stephen Logan will be our floor manager in the Capitol for the election. He has devoted himself to our campaign, and put his heart into electing Lincoln to the Senate."

"I will enter as the leading candidate," I declared. "We are in a strong position for the balloting. I can't thank you all enough."

The worst snowstorm since the winter of 1831 delayed the election for two weeks, but on the afternoon of February 8, 1855, in the Hall of Representatives, the legislators met to choose a United States senator.

Dressed for the occasion, hundreds of guests filled the galleries of the large room. Molly joined her dear friend Julia Trumbull in the front row. George Washington looked down on the proceedings from his life-sized portrait on the east wall of the Hall. The legislators sat at desks laid out in semi-circular rows on the floor.

When I met with Davis before the balloting, we both estimated that my vote total would be 47 or 48, just short of a majority.

With a rap of the gavel, the voting began.

When his name was called, a state representative or a state senator rose and called out the name of the candidate for whom he was voting. It did not take long.

On the first ballot, I received 45 votes, Shields had 41, Trumbull had 5, and Matteson had 1.

The one vote for Matteson kept us off guard, and raised the possibility the Democrats knew Shields could not win, and were waiting for the appropriate moment to switch those votes to the governor.

My advisors huddled with me during the break after the first ballot. They were concerned that the five votes for Trumbull: Norman Judd, Burton Cook, Henry Baker, George Allen, and John Palmer, were the men whose votes I needed to win. Trumbull was strongly anti-Nebraska and not popular with the pro-Nebraska/Douglas wing of the Democratic Party. In trying to pry those votes loose from Trumbull, we encountered the serious problem we had known all along.

In all likelihood they would not vote for a Whig, even if it was I whom they all knew and liked.

We would have to see where we stood after the second ballot.

The results were 43 votes for me, 41 for Shields, 6 for Trumbull, and 1 for Matteson.

Although I had lost two votes, I was not discouraged. If we could hold on to forty votes or more, there was still a chance to attract the votes I needed to win. I did have to admit that by this point the key legislators were not likely to change their votes, but if the balloting extended into the night, and possibly the following day, anything could happen.

Unfortunately the fourth ballot showed a trend that did not augur well for me. My total dipped to 38 votes, which indicated my support was slipping. Shields remained at 41 votes, and Trumbull's total almost doubled to 11. He gained the votes that I lost.

After the sixth ballot, there was stirring on the floor. Something was afoot. Billy, Swett, Davis, and I gathered in a corner of the room and awaited word from Logan.

We could see him in animated conversation with several of the legislators.

Finally, looking deeply concerned, he broke away and darted toward us.

"It's what we thought might happen," gasped Logan. "On the next ballot the Democrats who are voting for Shields will switch their votes to Governor Matteson. If they can pick up six anti-Nebraska votes from Trumbull, they will win."

"Not necessarily," I said firmly. "It will turn into a general scramble where anyone might win. Hold steady, and let our men know we are still in."

"Bravo!" cried Davis.

Our words buoyed Logan, who rushed back into the crowd.

It was on the eighth ballot I realized I would not win. The anti-Nebraska and Free Soil Democrats, who had supported me, were switching to Trumbull.

When I knew I had lost, my spirits sank, but I told myself I'd think about it later. No one had reached a majority, and we might yet influence the outcome. I saw how the pieces could fall into place, but each time Logan reported back to us, they had taken a different turn. I needed to steady myself for the moment I might have to make a difficult decision.

When Matteson came within four votes of victory on the ninth ballot, we huddled to consider the alternatives.

Davis began, "We are down to the question of what we think about Matteson winning."

"On the surface," observed Billy, "Matteson is a reasonable choice. It comes down to the question of whether we can trust him. I've talked to Palmer, who says he's genuinely anti-slavery, and anti-Douglas, but he can't confirm that Matteson has stated he's an anti-Nebraska man. He's so likable that no one questions whether he is trying to have it both ways, but with Matteson there is always a hint of corruption."

Swett took us in another direction. "If we do nothing, it's clear Matteson will win on the next ballot. It's really between Matteson and Trumbull. We hold the decisive votes."

Davis weighed in, "Most people don't like Trumbull. He's a cold fish. The one thing we can say for him is that he has been a steady anti-Nebraska man. Douglas can't stand him, which is another point in his favor."

I realized we had to make a decision. If Matteson was not reliable as an anti-Nebraska man, Trumbull definitely was. Davis was right. Trumbull was aloof and ambitious. I had known him as the husband of Julia Jayne, Molly's best friend. I knew him as a man of principle.

Davis advised me, "Lincoln, you have 15 votes. If you ask your men to vote for Trumbull, he will reach a majority. If you do not give your men those instructions, Matteson will win on the next ballot. You have to make the choice."

"Are you certain my men will vote for Trumbull if we give them the word?"

"Although they are steadfast for you, Lincoln, I do believe that they will do as you tell them."

I thought about it briefly, and then I told him, "Tell them it is my desire that they vote for Trumbull on the next ballot."

Logan was distraught after having invested so much hope and effort in the vote. He began to weep. Here was the second partner in my law career, the man who was most responsible for my growth as a lawyer, one of the men whom I most respected, in tears because I had lost the election. He had given his all to see me elected.

I did my best to console and thank him. He couldn't forgive Judd and Palmer, whom he felt had deceived him. They were among the five Trumbull voters on the first ballot whose support for him never wavered.

I was still too raw to give way to my emotions. I knew I would have to congratulate Trumbull, and that Molly would be both saddened and angry. I could hear her saying, "You had 45 and he had 5. How could he have won? I will never speak to them again." While dealing with my own disappointment, I would have to help her with the anger and resentment she would feel.

When the last ballot concluded and Trumbull was announced as the winner, the crowd in the galleries and just outside the hall erupted into cheers and huzzahs for Trumbull. It was a stunning victory for the anti-Nebraska coalition, and a strong rebuke to Douglas in his home state. If there was any solace in the early evening, it was in picturing the Little Giant in the Senate with a thorn in his side: Lyman Trumbull, who was one of his fiercest opponents, and now the other United States senator from his home state.

After supper, Molly and I sat disconsolately by the fireplace.

Neither of us said very much. She was angry, and I was still in disbelief.

Finally she spoke, "You had 45 votes and he had 5. How could he possibly have beaten you? Was there something more you should have done?"

I hoped I didn't look as downcast as I felt.

"My dear Molly, I am just as disappointed as you. I'm beginning to feel my fate is to fall short each time."

"I do not agree. I think you should challenge Douglas in the next election."

I looked at her with astonishment. Was she trying to rouse me from my lethargy? After the events of this day, it sounded like a joke.

"Whatever made you think of that?"

"Husband, do not doubt me. I know Illinois politics as well as you."

"Yes, you do, but if I can't defeat Shields or Matteson or Trumbull, how will I fare against Douglas?"

"I do not know, but you are the only man who can defeat him, and I believe you will."

I was too exhausted to give this any thought, so I rose from my chair and walked up the stairs to prepare for bed.

The following morning, the loss of the election hurt even more. No one had been better served by his team than I had been by mine, but the result of all our effort was nothing—just another loss.

Was fate toying with me? What could possibly be a road forward after this? My friends could not be expected to rally once more for me. How much longer could they believe in me? This had to be the last time I would run for office.

I contented myself with the honor of having been the first choice of a large majority of the 51 members who finally elected Trumbull. They had to surrender to Trumbull's smaller number, in order to prevent the election of Matteson, which would have been a Douglas victory. A less good-humored man than I, perhaps would not have consented to it—and it would not have been done without my consent. I could not, however, let the whole political result go to ruin, on a point merely personal to myself.

It was agonizing to have come so close. A week before the election, there was a moment when I thought we were within two votes of victory. Should I be angry and bitter about Judd's duplicity? He said he was willing to defy his party and take the consequences. In the end he couldn't do it.

I'd have to forgive him since I didn't harbor enmity toward anyone. It wasn't in my nature. When Molly and I attended the party honoring the Trumbulls, I was asked by John Palmer if I was still disappointed.

I replied, "Not too disappointed to congratulate my friend Trumbull," and went over to shake Trumbull's hand.

Later that morning, I walked over to the office to commiserate with Billy. He was my balm for moments like this one.

When I opened the door, who should I see sitting with my partner, but our jolly friend Davis. I assumed he had returned to Bloomington, but he slept over in Springfield and had stopped by to see me.

"If it isn't Lincoln, raised from the dead," he bellowed at me.

"We've been chatting," added Billy, "and we hoped you'd drop by before Davis departed. He plans to leave late this afternoon for Mount Pulaski."

"Lincoln, I am going to kidnap you, and we are going for a long walk. You have no choice."

Davis was fond of walking, and I was delighted to join him.

As we began, he said, "Today we will take the walk up to the Sangamon River. Although I grew up by the ocean, I find rivers equally soothing, and if there's anyone who needs some soothing today, it's us!"

It was February, but a winter thaw had arrived, and the day was warm. There was a hint of spring in the air. A light breeze tickled the branches of the birch trees that grew out over the road. A flock of sparrows flew overhead.

Davis asked, "And how are you feeling about the events of yesterday?"

"It hurts badly," I replied.

"Well, it should," he said, "but are you discouraged?"

"How can I not be? We were so sure of it. I've never wanted anything so much, and we were so close."

"Well, my friend, you may feel that fate has turned against you, but I am not so sure."

"But you and Logan, both of you, and all the others who helped, how can they not abandon me?"

"We continue to believe in you, Lincoln, and we believe you should challenge Douglas for his Senate seat in 1858."

I was astounded to hear this.

"Why, that's just what Molly told me this morning."

"Well, she knows as much about Illinois politics as you or I do."

"That's just what she said."

"She is a smart woman, and she believes in your future."

"How can I beat Douglas when I couldn't prevail yesterday?"

"You are the man to do it. You understand him. You've known him for twenty years. You know his weak spots, and he's deathly afraid of you."

"I don't believe that."

"You have crafted a thoughtful position on slavery. You are a gifted orator. You are the person to take us Whigs into a fusion party. Douglas has put all his eggs into the Kansas-Nebraska basket, and it's about to come a cropper. Someone has to stop him. You are the one."

I didn't respond, and we walked along the riverbank in silence for a while.

Davis broke it by asking, "Lincoln, how is your domestic life?"

"I have to say it has improved. Molly was more temperamental after we lost Eddie, but with the births of the younger boys, and our immersion back into Illinois politics, she's been a fine companion."

Watching the current sweep down the channel, my thoughts turned meditative.

"It is near here that Molly and I agreed to marry," I said. "That was a time of possibility, but now, as I see this river, I cannot help but think of all the hopes it has swept away."

"Our little ones," Davis said while looking down into the river.

"They are always with us," I replied. "I still think of little Eddie several times a day."

"Do you remember what you did for us when young Lucy died?"

"I gave George a seat in my buggy so you and Sarah could ride together in yours. George was eight, the same age as Bob, so I knew what stories to tell him."

Davis spoke slowly, "Yes, Lucy died in August, and it was better for Sarah to be with us on the circuit than to stay at home."

Content for our afternoon of companionship, we walked back to Springfield, and Davis trotted away in his buggy for Mount Pulaski.

A few nights later I had another strange dream. I was never upset by a dream, but some of them begged for explanation. It was hard to know the border between what was revelatory and what was absurd.

I was intensely aware of being alone.

It was cold, frightfully cold, and I could not recognize the place. It was night, and the wind swirled a dense gray fog around me. I could barely see, but I could hear waves breaking on what must have been the shore.

The sound rose toward me. Was I standing somewhere above it? I could not tell.

The cold air cut into my face, but I was covered by a thick black cape. Underneath the cape, belted to my side, was a long scabbard sheltering a sword. I could now see that I stood on a stone passageway.

The fog lifted slightly, and I could see a wall surrounding me. There were spaces cut into the stonework at the top. I peered through one of them and could see that we were looking down onto the ocean.

Then I heard voices and saw a long line of human shapes, covered in black shawls, walking on the seashore. I could barely make out what they were saying, but it sounded like, "Help us, save us, avenge us!"

And then from the night sky, I faintly heard a thin voice calling, " . . . to lay down his life for his friends."

Chapter 9

I Felt as If I Were Riding the Wind

As I gradually healed from the loss of the Senate election, I continued to dedicate myself to my law practice. The internal improvements for which I fought as a state legislator in the 1830s came to fruition in the 1850s. Cases involving railroads and steamboats became more complex and lucrative for lawyers. Billy and I were retained for several of these cases, but in the summer and fall of 1855, the case that piqued my interest most intensely was the patent infringement suit that Cyrus McCormick brought against John H. Manny.

McCormick became famous as the inventor of the reaper, the machine that helped to harvest crops. By 1855, the McCormick factory in Chicago produced the most reapers in the world. When Manny first began manufacturing reapers in Rockport in 1847, he was no threat to McCormick. By 1854, however, Manny had become a major competitor. In November 1854, McCormick brought suit against Manny in Chicago. He alleged patent infringement for the divider, which came before the sickle and separated the grain shoots, as well as the reel post behind the cutter.

Manny's attorney was George Harding of Philadelphia, who chose Edwin M. Stanton of Pittsburgh to be his co-counsel. Because the case was scheduled for trial in Chicago, Harding felt an Illinois lawyer would be an important addition to his team. He sent an associate, Peter Watson, to interview me. I learned later that when Watson visited Molly and me in Springfield, he was not impressed, but with their need for a local attorney and sensing that I might be miffed if I wasn't chosen, he acceded to Harding's wish. I was sent a retainer of $400 and led to believe I would be delivering the closing argument.

In the meantime, a new presiding judge was chosen, and the venue for the trial was moved to Cincinnati. Although their need for me diminished, I was still told to prepare my brief.

When I was in Chicago on other business in July, I went out to Rockford, and spent half a day studying and examining Manny's machine. Planning to devote some time to the case in August, I wrote Watson that I needed copies of the bill and answer and the depositions. When I never heard from him, I began to wonder whether something was amiss.

Nonetheless, my preparation was more diligent than normal because I would be contending with some of the most eminent lawyers in the country.

I arrived in Cincinnati on September 18 as the trial would begin on the 20th.

On the following day, I walked to the Burnet House where Stanton and Harding were staying. The first thing I learned was that Stanton, a man with supreme confidence in his legal skills, had taken over as chief counsel. A determined man with an abrupt manner, he was used to being in charge. He peered at me through small rimmed glasses, and when he took my measure, he looked over at Harding with disgust. They were dressed in well-tailored suits, and I surmised that my ill-fitting clothing had not made a good first impression.

As we started on the walk from the hotel to the courthouse, I tried to lighten the conversation by saying, "Let's go over there in a gang."

Stanton whispered to Harding, "Let that fellow go with his gang. We'll walk together. I can't get away from that giraffe fast enough."

When we reached the courtroom, Stanton announced that he and Harding would give the arguments in the case, and that I would have a minimal role. After the trial was moved from Chicago to Cincinnati, they foresaw I would not be needed, but their strategy was to keep me involved lest I desert them for the other side.

I decided to stay in Cincinnati and attend the trial sessions. If nothing else, it was a chance to watch outstanding lawyers in a landmark case. When I gave Harding an envelope with the documents I had prepared for the case, he returned it unopened. Stanton wouldn't walk or talk with me. I overheard him saying to Harding, "Why is that long-armed baboon still around?" I stayed until the verdict, which was delivered in favor of Manny.

When I returned to Springfield on the train, I had to admit how shabbily they had treated me, but if someone was petty with me, that didn't mean I should be petty in return.

I was surprised to receive a $600 check from Harding for services rendered on the case, but I returned it to him. When he sent it again, I decided to keep it.

Throughout 1855 and into 1856, the friends who became my political advisors during the Senate election continued to meet with me each month. Since I had no active political plans, it was more to monitor state and national politics. David Davis kept pressing me to run against Douglas in 1858, but I was tender about the likelihood of losing another election. What most occupied our attention was the chaos engulfing Kansas.

It was what I predicted in my Peoria speech. Douglas's idea of popular sovereignty opened the Kansas territory to a contest for control of the state legislature. Whichever side, pro-slavery or anti-slavery, could enlist more voters would win.

William H. Seward, the anti-slavery senator from New York, declared, "Come on then, Gentlemen of the Slave States, since there is no escaping your challenge, I accept it on behalf of the cause of freedom. We will engage in competition for the virgin soil of Kansas, and God give the victory to the side which is stronger in numbers as it is in right."

Beginning in the summer of 1854, settlers from both sides emigrated to Kansas to become residents. Rumors spread of large groups of abolitionists coming to Kansas. In response, pro-slavery "border ruffians" from Missouri rushed into the territory. One of their leaders, Senator David Atchison, proclaimed that he wanted "to kill every God-damned abolitionist in the district." Their numbers swelled when it was time for voting. This strategy helped them prevail in the first legislative election in March of 1855. The representatives met as the territorial government and passed harsh laws protecting slavery.

Claiming the election to be fraudulent, the free-state men voted in December to establish a territorial government in Topeka and approved their own free-state constitution. By the end of 1855, the territory of Kansas was split into two factions with rival governments seated in Lecompton and Topeka.

The inevitable next step was for both sides to arm themselves. For the free-state faction, rifles began to arrive from New England. The congregation of the Reverend Henry Ward Beecher, Harriet Beecher Stowe's brother, sent rifles to Kansas that became known as "Beecher's Bibles." The pro-slavery men from Missouri were armed when they crossed the border into Kansas.

After the severe winter of 1856, in the spring the two sides began to skirmish. Violence over slavery had begun in Kansas.

It was a good time for my friends and me to gather at David Davis's office in Bloomington. We needed to meet because we were being asked to became part of a group of anti-slavery men working to build a new political party in Illinois.

The Kansas-Nebraska Act in 1854 brought about a remarkable transformation of the political parties in America—in the country and in individual states. The Whig Party split into Northern Whigs, who generally opposed the Kansas-Nebraska Act because it allowed the expansion of slavery, and Southern Whigs who favored it for that very reason. This division caused the party to collapse. The Democrats, strong in the South, retained enough support in the North to form a governing coalition. Anti-Nebraska Democrats were courted by the remnants of the Whig Party in the North. The rise of the Know Nothings complicated the picture.

I wrote to my friend Joshua Speed in August 1855, "You enquire where I now stand. That is a disputed point. I think I am a whig; but others say there are no whigs, and that I am an abolitionist. When I was at Washington I voted for the Wilmot Proviso as good as forty times, and I never heard of anyone attempting to unwhig me for that. I now do no more than oppose the extension of slavery."

In February 1856, several anti-slavery newspaper editors met in Decatur and attempted to unite the opponents of slavery into a political party. I was invited to the meeting as a guest, but I soon found myself in the thick of the discussions. It took me back to my days in the legislature when I was a young man. So much of our work was patching together legislation from competing interests. My moderate views on most controversies made that possible. Now, I was once again in the middle on most issues, but firm on the one or two that defined our cause.

By the end of the day, we had hammered out a platform. We began with the premise that freedom was our fundamental national principle, and slavery was an institution localized in the South. We opposed the extension of slavery and favored restoring the Missouri Compromise. We recognized the Fugitive Slave Act must be upheld, and that the constitution protected slavery where it already existed. In opposition to the nativists, we supported the immigration laws.

The platform was adopted, a central committee created, and a call issued for a state convention in Bloomington on May 29,1856. I was delighted that Billy was nominated to serve on the central committee. When issues were percolating, he could keep me informed.

We rode back from Decatur to Springfield by train. He and I had grown closer over the years. Not only had he become an able lawyer, but we now shared equal credit for the success of our law practice. We navigated the age difference between us, and he became a valuable colleague, a good friend, and a trusted political advisor. In Illinois political circles, Billy could speak for me.

On the train trip back, we talked about the successful meetings in Decatur and the new friends we'd made. The clickity-clack from the train wheels moving along the rails relaxed us, and soon we were pleasantly reading. I pulled a newspaper out of my valise, and Billy settled back with a thin volume of poetry. He was more widely read, and he loved poetry as much as I did.

Billy couldn't refrain from interrupting me and said, "Lincoln, Parker has sent me this collection of poems he was given by Emerson. It's by somebody completely unknown. Walt Whitman is his name. It's radically different from anything I've seen before.

"Listen to this."

I dropped the paper into my lap and reluctantly listened to his recitation.

"The runaway slave came to my house and stopped outside,

I heard his motions crackling the twigs of the woodpile,

Through the swung half-door of the kitchen I saw him limpsey and weak,

And went where he sat on a log, and led him in and assured him,

And brought water and filled a tub for his sweated body and bruised feet,

And gave him a room that entered from my own, and gave him some coarse clean clothes,

And remember perfectly well his revolving eyes and his awkwardness,

And remember putting plasters on the galls of his neck and ankles;

He staid with me a week before he was recuperated and passed north,

I had him sit next me at table . . . . my firelock leaned in the corner."

"What do you think?" he asked.

"It's unusual," I replied.

When I returned to Bloomington in the afternoon of May 28, I was greeted warmly in David Davis's office by Leonard Swett, Billy who had come on an earlier train, and Davis himself.

With dark wooden paneling, a large roll-top desk, and leather arm chairs, Davis's office was plusher and cozier than ours. In addition to being a lawyer, a judge, and a politician, Davis was becoming a wealthy businessman. Investing in land brought him fruitful returns.

"Lincoln," he said while easing himself into his comfortable desk chair, "it turns out we both were right. Kansas is in flames, and popular sovereignty is becoming Douglas's downfall."

"It's actually getting worse," said Swett, holding up a *New York Tribune* headline for all of us to see:

"THE TOWN OF LAWRENCE IN ASHES!"

"Read us what has happened," exclaimed Billy.

Swett put on his glasses and read from a front page article by a *Tribune* correspondent. "Sheriff Jones and his posse commenced their work of destruction immediately by throwing the two printing presses and type into the river. This being done, they began to cannonade the hotel and fire by platoons at the same time at the windows; meanwhile the women and children fleeing in every direction, the Sheriff having refused any time to remove them or property to a place of safety, as he said they might have done it before had they wanted to do so. As I was leaving town there were several who wanted to know where they could find a place of safety but I could offer no consolation. I, being mounted, succeeded in getting away after a long chase. I left the vicinity about 8 p.m. When I was 15 miles distant, I could see the flames of what appeared to be a large fire in the direction of Lawrence, and have no doubt but that the town is in ashes and many of its inhabitants butchered."

"Who is Sheriff Jones?" asked Billy.

Swett replied, "He's the pro-slavery sheriff of Douglas County."

"This is the work of those border ruffians, and it is villainous," added Davis. "First it was skirmishing, and now it's come to open warfare. All because of Douglas's presidential ambitions. How can one man be allowed to hold this country hostage? I tell you, Lincoln, he is vulnerable in '58."

"I'm not as certain as you, Davis," I said, "although I'm a bit more interested in it than I was last year. If the anti-slavery groups coalesce into one party, there could be a substantial anti-Douglas bloc in this state."

Swett put down the paper, and Billy picked it up and started reading it. While we were talking pleasantries, Billy broke in with alarm, "Here's something else. Wait till you hear this!"

"By the news from Washington it will be seen that Senator Sumner has been savagely and brutally assaulted, while sitting in his seat in the Senate chamber, by the Hon. Mr. Brooks of South Carolina. The particulars show that Mr. Sumner was struck unawares over the head by a loaded cane and stunned, and then the ruffianly attack was continued with many blows, the Hon. Mr. Keith of South Carolina keeping any of those around, who might be so disposed, from attempting a rescue. No meaner exhibition of Southern cowardice—generally called Southern chivalry—was ever witnessed."

We were astonished by what Billy had read.

Davis rose, and shaking with emotion, he cried out, "What is happening to our country? Our institutions are being strained to the point of breaking. Where is all this going?"

None of us ventured a response. Between the sack of Lawrence and the attack on Sumner, we were stunned into silence.

Billy and I stayed in Bloomington through May 29, and together with Swett and Davis attended the first convention of the Republican Party in Illinois.

The key issue on the eve of the convention was whether we could pull together the different elements of the Whig Party in Illinois. Could we balance the abolitionists in the North with the moderates in the center and conservatives in the South? If that were possible, could we then bring in the anti-Nebraska Democrats, the Free Soilers, most of whom were anti-slavery Democrats, and the nativists who were willing to forsake their bigotry? Would they all be able to put aside their differences and join together to form a new political party?

We would find out the next day.

My only official duty was to chair the committee on nominations, but all the disparate groups welcomed me to negotiate among them. I spent the morning with them all and was able to work out acceptable compromises. By the afternoon we had built a set of principles upon which the new party would stand.

The first one was that Congress had the power to prohibit slavery in the territories; and while we recognized the constitutional rights of the South, we held the principles expressed in the Declaration of Independence, and our national constitution, required that power should be exerted to prevent the extension of slavery into the territories.

Additional ones were condemning the violence in Kansas, urging that the Missouri Compromise be restored, calling for Kansas to enter the Union as a free state, vowing to support the constitution and the Union, and disapproving of nativist prejudice.

That afternoon, we dispensed with more party business, and in the evening the speeches began. Mine was scheduled to be last.

Unlike my Peoria speech, I had not prepared a text. I had given so many speeches after Peoria, and I was so familiar with the issues, that the words simply flowed from me. I was deeply passionate about the principles of the new party, which we finally agreed to name officially the Republican Party.

I spoke for ninety minutes. Once I had my rhythm, the pieces fit together. We could not allow slavery to expand. I was certain this was the intention of the Founding Fathers. Our democratic experiment, the noblest government on earth, could not be allowed to perish.

The Union must be preserved in the purity of its principles as well as in the integrity of its territorial parts. The Kansas-Nebraska Act should never have been passed by Congress. Douglas's policy of popular sovereignty, which was supposed to end slavery agitation, had enflamed it. Kansas was in chaos and at war because the rival factions were ready to kill each other over the slavery issue. The platform of the Republican Party was a plan to end slavery gradually.

I wove all my themes from the past two years into the speech and celebrated our achievement of giving birth to the Republican Party in Illinois.

As I continued to speak I felt more impassioned than ever before. Sweat was dripping down my face, and the words continued to flow. I felt as if I were riding the wind. By the light of the bubbling gas lamps, I could see that the reporters and the stenographers had stopped writing. They were just listening.

When I finished, wave after wave of applause thundered through the arena. I was exhausted, but I acknowledged the acclamation of the crowd. I had never felt such a demonstration of enthusiasm and good will from any audience. The ovation continued. I was deeply gratified by their response. I knew the energy they were transferring to me would sustain me in the days ahead.

I descended the rostrum and greeted the crowd, many of whom were my good friends. They slapped my back and prepared to carry me out of the hall.

Davis was motioning me to have a word with him.

"Lincoln, he cried, "that was the greatest speech anyone has ever given in Illinois."

"Thank you, thank you," I yelled back to him above the din.

When we were finally together, he cupped his hand and shouted into my ear, "Lincoln, you are their leader. The Senate nomination in '58 is yours if you want it."

"I'll give it some thought," I replied.

The next morning Billy and I boarded the train back to Springfield. We were both exhausted, but before we could doze, he asked, "Did you see the papers this morning?"

"No, my friend, I didn't have time."

"There is news from Kansas."

"What has happened now?"

"It's alarming!"

"Well, for heaven's sake, tell me what has happened."

"There's been a massacre. It was bloody."

"Well, Greeley has called it 'Bleeding Kansas' so it can't be any worse than what's been reported already."

"It is."

I was becoming a bit irritated with him, and said, "Out with it, Billy"

"Well, it has to do with a fellow named John Brown. He's been a bit of a ne'er do well, but he's always hated slavery. Finally he decided to do something about it.

"Brown and five of his sons came to Kansas to keep it free. They joined a free-state volunteer group known as the Pottawatomie Rifles, and their mission was to defend Lawrence against an attack from the pro-slavery vigilantes.

"They did not get to Lawrence in time to stop Sheriff Jones from sacking it.

"Brown was dismayed and led seven men, including four of his sons, on an anti-slavery rampage. They were armed with rifles and broadswords. Late at night they broke into the cabin of a pro-slavery settler named James Doyle, forced him outside, and then returned to take the two oldest sons. The mother asked for mercy, and they spared her and a younger son.

"Brown's men used their swords to split open the heads of the three men, and Brown himself shot Doyle to make sure he was dead. After this, they hacked the bodies and mutilated them.

"From there, they entered the cabin of Allen Wilkinson, a pro-slavery legislator, and despite pleas from his wife, took him out, split open his skull, and tore apart his body.

"Finally, at the cabin of another pro-slavery man, James Harris, they grabbed a house guest, cut his skull in half, ran their swords though his side, and cut off his hand.

"Then they left and returned to the Pottawatomie Rifle Company."

By the time Billy finished, I had covered my face with my hands.

When I dropped my forearms, I looked at him and said, "Oh, Billy, Davis was right. It will now be war in Kansas. It is Douglas who is responsible for all this bloodshed."

On June 17, 1856, I attended the Republican national convention in Philadelphia. Our presidential nominee was John C. Fremont, the noted explorer of the West. On the first ballot for a vice-presidential candidate, 110 votes, enough for second place, were cast for Lincoln, but I assumed it was Levi Lincoln of Massachusetts. The votes were actually for me. Walter L. Dayton of New Jersey was chosen on the second ballot.

The Democrats nominated James Buchanan for president. He won the election in November. We were written off as a sectional party, with appeal to some voters in the North and West. The Democrats held the South and won several states in the North. For them, it was a working majority.

Chapter 10

A House Divided Against Itself Cannot Stand

We were just about to turn right onto Edwards Street when Willie cried, "Papa! Tad has fallen out of the wagon!"

I looked up from the book I'd been reading as I wheeled the boys around the neighborhood in their wooden wagon, and, sure enough, there was no Tad. He must have tumbled off when I'd been preoccupied with Byron's poetry and Willie was daydreaming.

Here was a fine mystery. We needed to find him before Molly or one of the neighbors heard about this. I could hear her shrieking, "Taddie is lost! Taddie will die!"

I rolled the wagon a little farther, and then turned around to see if Willie was still there.

"William Wallace Lincoln, this is worse than the time you ran away from me when I was trying to give you a bath. You ran down the stairs and out into the street naked. I finally caught you running up the path to Jameson Jenkins's house."

"Papa, you know I hate a bath, even when you give it to me."

"Well, we came through that one unscathed, but I wonder where that little codger could have gone."

The Reverend Francis Springer walked by on the way back to his house on the corner of Eighth and Jackson. We were relieved that he gave us a brief greeting and then moved on. Still, we were worried that he might find Tad before we did.

"There he is!" Willie exclaimed as I turned around to see Tad stretched out on the grass in front of the Dubois house. He was picking dandelions.

We were fortunate he wasn't crying.

"Let's roll him right back in," I said to Willie, "and then we'll head up to Corneau and Diller's Drugstore to get some candy. Maybe that will stop him from spilling the beans."

Willie looked up and smiled, glad to be in on something with me, and with the prospect of chocolate cream drops or a lemon lollipop.

In the evening, Molly and I relaxed together in our chairs by the fireplace. The boys were asleep upstairs. Two of our cats were purring on the hearth rug, and a third was curled up in my lap.

"Will you challenge Douglas?" asked Molly.

"The others think I should. The Republican Party has unified, and they want me to be the nominee."

"And what do you think?" she asked.

"I want to know what you think."

"You must defeat him. You are the only one who can do it. You must stand up against the pro-slavery group that is gaining control of our country."

Looking directly at her, I declared, "I have decided to run against him."

She was delighted, but I had to tell her, "Something happened today that changes everything. The Supreme Court has ruled on Dred Scott."

"You thought it might be coming."

"I did, particularly when Buchanan mentioned it in his inaugural address."

"What did they decide?"

"They decreed that Scott had no rights because a negro cannot be a citizen. They ruled that Congress has no power to keep slavery from expanding into the territories. They ruled the Missouri Compromise was unconstitutional, and since Scott's claim for freedom was based on his residence in Wisconsin, it was null and void. They returned Dred Scott to his owner."

Molly looked shocked.

"This is unconscionable!" she said. "This is the work of Taney and the other southern justices. It's a step toward making slavery a national and not a regional institution. It will make popular sovereignty meaningless. It must be overruled."

"I will take some time to read it closely."

"What will you do?"

"Sadly we have to accept it, but you are right, we must work to overrule it. That might be hard with five justices from the South on the court, but we must try. At least Justices McLean and Curtis voted against it. I will see how Douglas responds."

"What will he say?"

"He will support it, but I suspect he will try to find some way around it to preserve popular sovereignty."

Douglas responded to the Dred Scott decision on June 7, 1857, in the State Capitol at Springfield. Molly and I were in the audience.

He did support the court's decision, particularly Taney's assertion that the negro had no rights.

He was delighted by the court's ruling that the Missouri Compromise was unconstitutional. For him, it confirmed the validity of his decision to repeal it in the Kansas-Nebraska Act.

I was also right that he would try to weasel his way around part of the court's ruling. To maintain the integrity of popular sovereignty, he stated that the people of a territory could exclude slavery. He said the settler's right to take slaves into a territory was a "barren and worthless right, unless sustained, protected, and enforced by appropriate police regulations and local legislation."

I was surprised by this and made a mental note of it.

On the evening of June 26, I replied to Douglas in the same chamber in which he had spoken two weeks earlier.

I stated I would not stand with those who would not comply with the Dred Scott decision. Under the constitution, the rulings of the Supreme Court were to be upheld. With that I concurred, but it did not mean we could not do all within our power to overturn the decision. I outlined the points where I felt the decision was in error.

Douglas insisted that I favored complete racial equality. He claimed, "Republicans want to vote, and eat, and sleep, and marry with negroes."

To this I replied, "Now I protest against that counterfeit logic which concludes that, because I do not want a black woman for a slave I must necessarily want her for a wife. I need not have her for either. I can just leave her alone. In some respects she certainly is not my equal; but in her natural right to eat the bread she earns with her own hands without asking leave of any one else, she is my equal, and the equal of all others."

In early July, after breakfast with Molly and the boys, I walked to my office. As ever, Billy had already been there since 7 a.m., and he greeted me cheerfully.

He looked up at me, and with some urgency said, "Lincoln, our plates are full this morning!"

The metaphor was a clumsy one, so I tried to humor him by saying, "Well, Billy, let's start with the main course, shall we say the beef? Is it politics or the law?"

"It's both today."

"Two main courses? Then I should agree with you that our plates are indeed full, and if it's the Effie Alton case, if we win, our plates will be full for a year."

"There's a letter from the U.S. circuit court in Chicago this morning," he said. "Effie Alton goes to trial in September."

"We will be ready. You know I've spent ample time at the site of the accident where the steamboat crashed into the bridge pillar. I've studied the bridge carefully, the amount of rail and steamboat traffic over and under the bridge, the condition of the steamboat and the incompetence of her captain, and the egregious expense for the railroads of digging a tunnel under the river or building a suspension bridge above it."

He replied, "I know you have been preparing for this one for over a year."

"We will be ready," I repeated.

"Then perhaps we should turn to the politics," he advised.

"If it involves Douglas, I suspect it will be the spinach."

"But that's a side course and not a main one."

"All right, let's call it the catfish."

"Yes, that's it!" he cried. "This morning's papers report that Douglas has taken a stand on Lecompton."

"That's the pro-slavery constitution for Kansas that was written after the anti-slavery men refused to vote?"

"Right, even though they outnumbered the pro-slavery men, they felt the election was fraudulent," answered Billy.

"And where is Buchanan in this?"

"Doughface that he is and beholden to the South for his election, he supports the Lecompton constitution. Kansas has now applied for statehood, and Buchanan wants Congress to admit it as a slave state."

"I'll bet that has set off a row."

"The North is enraged, and the Democrats are divided over it."

"What about Douglas?"

"Here's the surprise: Douglas has broken with Buchanan over Lecompton. He is attacking the president for violating the doctrine of popular sovereignty. The vote was fraudulent, and Buchanan is accepting it as the basis for admitting Kansas into the Union. Douglas is livid and is willing to split the Democratic Party."

"Surely he must have some ulterior motive," I observed.

"I'm afraid so. He's thinking ahead to the Senate race next year. If he endorses Lecompton, he's worried that he could lose the election."

"That would have been good for me!"

"True, but for one problem that the papers are citing today. Douglas may seek support from the Republican Party now that he has defied Buchanan. There is even some speculation that he might become a Republican."

"You can't be serious."

"Listen to this. Greeley wrote an editorial in the *New York Tribune*. He praised Douglas by saying, 'His course has not been merely right—it has been conspicuously, courageous, eminently so.'"

"If Douglas becomes a Republican, all is lost," I said angrily. "He is such a schemer that I can't believe the Republicans would accept him."

"They would if they think he can win."

"Billy, we must never sell old friends to buy old enemies."

The threat of Douglas becoming a Republican hung over us for several months. Some of the eastern Republicans proposed that our Republican Party of Illinois should not run a candidate against Douglas in the senate race. This incensed me and many of my friends in Illinois.

Billy sent a letter to Elihu Washburne, who was reputed to be waffling on the issue.

In it he wrote, "We want to govern ourselves in our own way. We want the man that we want, and have him and him alone. Illinois is not for sale. If the Republicans of Illinois were to run Douglas for the Senate, the masses would drag us from power and grind us to powder. Douglas's abuse of us as Whigs—as Republicans—as men in society, and as individuals, has been so slanderous—dirty—low—long, and continuous, that we cannot soon forgive, and can never forget."

Billy decided to travel east to meet with Douglas and the Republicans who were promoting him. In Washington, Douglas told him, "Give Mr. Lincoln my regards when you return, and tell him I have crossed the river and burned my boat. The Republicans and I will be together soon."

Not to be deterred, he journeyed to New York, where he met with Horace Greeley. When Billy told Greeley,

"Douglas has abused and betrayed the North," Greeley urged him to forget the past.

When Billy returned to Springfield, he wrote Greeley a lengthy response with his final salvo, "Did Douglas ever give an inch in his whole political life? He is the most imperious and selfish man in America. He is the greatest liar in the world."

What saved me was the good turn I did for Trumbull in yielding my votes to him in the Senate contest of 1855. The leaders of our party in Illinois cited this in discussions of whether to encourage Douglas. Their perception was that I had earned the nomination by putting party principles before personal ambition. I had also gained support by helping to build the coalition that became the Illinois Republican Party in May of 1856.

I would be running against Douglas for his Senate seat. No one would have imagined that. How far I'd come and how unpredictable events had been since 1854. I'd been certain my political career was over, but the Kansas-Nebraska Act stirred me out of my lethargy. All the reading I'd done, and the discussions I'd had with political friends and rivals, prepared me for this moment. My legal work, both inside and outside of court, had taught me to be more logical and precise. My thinking was deeper, my writing more elegant, and my orations more compelling. All this came from a power I sensed in myself that I had not known before. I'd developed a quiet confidence that I could contend with Senator Douglas.

As June 16, 1858, the date of the Republican state convention in Springfield, approached, I gathered with my advisors in our law office. Although the tight circle was bound to grow for the Senate campaign, for this meeting it remained Billy, David Davis, and Leonard Swett.

Davis opened the meeting by remarking, "Lincoln, it would appear the nomination is yours."

"I think so," I replied.

Billy added, "There are pockets of Republicans in the East and even here in Illinois who are still infatuated with Douglas, but we've put out the largest fires. Loyalty to Lincoln ran deep, and he will be nominated for the Senate race tomorrow."

Swett looked over at me and asked, "Will you give an acceptance speech?"

"I've been working on it all week. It's been coming to me late at night when I write at the little desk in my bedroom."

"Can you give us a preview?" asked Davis.

"This one has been more difficult," I replied. "I will have a prepared text, and I will read it. As you all know, that's unusual for me, but I want there to be no doubt about what I've said. It is shorter than some of my speeches, and I will read it slowly."

"Will you share it with us now?" asked Davis.

I walked over to my desk, rummaged through a few piles, found the text, and returned to my chair. Removing my glasses from my coat pocket, I placed them over my nose and ears, and began to read.

"Mr. President and Gentlemen of the Convention.

If we could first know where we are, and whither we are tending, we could then better judge what to do and how to do it.

We are now into the fifth year, since a policy was initiated with the avowed object, and confident promise, of putting an end to slavery agitation.

Under the operation of that policy, that agitation has not only, not ceased, but has constantly augmented.

In my opinion, it will not cease, until a crisis shall have been reached and passed.

A house divided against itself cannot stand.

I believe this government cannot endure, permanently half slave and half free.

I do not expect the Union to be dissolved—I do not expect the house to fall—but I do expect it will cease to be divided.

It will become all one thing, or all the other.

Either the opponents of slavery will arrest the further spread of it, and place it where the public mind shall rest in the belief that it is in course of ultimate extinction; or its advocates will push it forward till it shall become alike lawful in all the States, old as well as new—North as well as South.

"Let's stop there," I said.

There wasn't a sound.

I sat quietly, and so did the others.

Finally Swett broke the silence, "Lincoln, if you give that speech, you will be defeated in the Senate race. Douglas will tar you as a Black Republican and an abolitionist. He will charge that the Republicans want racial equality."

"He will accuse you of leading us into civil war," came an animated addition from Davis.

"I know that's what he'll say, but none of it is true."

"Billy, what do you think?" asked Swett.

"It's too radical for Illinois."

"Now you've heard from all of us," said Davis. "You will need to eliminate or tone down that part. It's almost like poetry; in fact, it's the best analysis of our national dilemma I've heard from anyone, but you can't use it."

"You have to think of your audience," added Swett.

"I have one question for you."

I looked them all in the eyes.

"Is it true?" I asked.

Each of them nodded his head.

"Gentlemen, I have heard you, but I am convinced the truth will prevail if we are both measured and bold. It is time for us to be resolute. I am going to give the speech as I read it to you."

I did give the "House Divided" speech to the cheering delegates in Representatives Hall. It was the first speech of the Senate campaign against Douglas. Next would come the political combat, and I was ready for the fight.

Chapter 11

It's a Slip and Not a Fall

On July 14, 1858, I asked Stephen Douglas to meet with me. He accepted my invitation, and a few days later, he joined me in the library at the State Capitol. It was the late evening, so we had the room to ourselves.

I was there first. He was half an hour late. He blew into the room and said he'd found it hard to leave a dinner party.

We both sat down at one of the sturdy tables near the gas light.

"Well, Lincoln," he roared, "whatever can you want of me?"

"I've been tardy," I replied, "in congratulating you on your marriage to Miss Cutts."

"I've been quite fortunate; she's a lovely girl—rather a great beauty. She's tidied up my house and my life. It's a big job, but she seems to enjoy it."

"I hear your house is now the center of the Washington social circle."

"Indeed, Adele is the ideal hostess. Martha was ill so often that she couldn't join me at all the Washington parties. As you know, that's where much of our business is done. Adele loves it. She's everybody's favorite, and she has a mind for politics."

"And the boys?"

"They adore her. She's taken them under her wing, and we are all together in Washington."

"Such good news, Judge!"

He looked impatient and barked at me, "Now, Lincoln, what is it you want of me?"

"I am now your opponent in this fall's Senate election."

"Yes, you are—as a representative of the Black Republican Party."

"Judge, I wonder if you'd be interested in debating me?"

He gave me a strange look, like a child with a piece that wouldn't fit into his wooden puzzle.

"But who would be foolish enough to debate me?"

"I would."

"Lincoln, you know what would happen to you. You'd be sliced like a Christmas ham. This must be one of Davis's schemes."

"As a matter of fact, it is," I countered.

"Lincoln, you'd be a sacrificial lamb. You served a disgraceful term in the House. I was there for two productive terms, and I'm a two-term senator, soon to be a third. You'd be in over your head. I've debated the likes of Clay and Webster while you've debated the local toadies of Sangamon County."

"Judge, we'd have a chance to debate the issues of the day."

"But, Lincoln, we agree on many of them."

"Not all."

"You've become a Black Republican abolitionist."

"Not so."

"Aha! Are you already running away from your 'House Divided' proclamation?"

"You can smear me all you like, Judge, but you know where I stand on slavery."

"I'd put you in a sausage grinder."

"What happened to your little flirtation with the Black Republican Party?" I asked him.

"Bah! Nothing but humbug."

"I wish you'd said that three months ago," I replied.

"Enough, Lincoln, I'd relish the chance to make hash out of you, once and for all. I'll tell my associates to await a visit from yours," he yelled and stormed out of the room.

Our advisors scheduled seven debates in towns up and down Illinois. They would begin on August 21 in Ottawa and end in Alton on October 15. The format for each debate was for one of us to speak for an hour, the other for an hour and a half, and the first speaker for a concluding thirty minutes. We were to alternate the order as the debates progressed.

Both the Judge and I had extensive speaking schedules throughout the summer, but interest in the campaign heightened as we approached the first debate.

August 21, the day for the first debate at Ottawa, finally arrived. It was steaming hot and oppressively humid, but by noon the crowd, mostly farmers, shopkeepers, and artisans and their families, had reached 10,000. The town was alive with festivities: brass bands, serenades by the party faithful, campaign parades for both the Judge and me, posters and flags hanging over stores and homes, an occasional round of artillery, and a cannon to announce the arrival of Judge Douglas. As we ascended to the platform with the speaker's rostrum, loud cheers rolled out from the crowd.

The debate was scheduled for two o'clock, but it was delayed because the rostrum began to sway. It was overflowing with spectators who had to be escorted off the platform.

Judge Douglas spoke first. He came at me like an express train.

His goal was to tar me as an abolitionist. Using a document which he claimed to be the platform of the Republican Party in Illinois, he cited it plank by plank, and asked me if I agreed with the propositions. To agree with them meant I was leaning toward abolition. To disagree meant I was repudiating the platform of my own party. I did not reply.

His next strategy was to portray me as an advocate of negro social and political equality.

"If you desire negro citizenship, if you desire to allow them to come into the state and settle with the white man, if you desire them to vote on an equality with yourselves, and to make them eligible to office, to serve on juries, and to judge your rights, then support Mr. Lincoln and the Black Republican Party."

The Judge attacked the position I took in my "House Divided" speech when I said, "I believe this government cannot endure, permanently half slave and half free."

"Why can it not exist divided into free and slave states? Washington, Franklin, Madison, Hamilton, Jay, and the great men of that day made this government divided into free and slave states. Why can it not exist on the same principles on which our fathers made it?"

These were the two main themes of his first hour, and he wove them into the rest of his presentation.

The Judge's arguments, delivered with his characteristic bombast, surprised me and put me immediately on the defensive. I tried to respond by quoting extensively from my Peoria speech. I tried to deflect his assault, but I never really got my footing in my ninety-minute rejoinder.

It was late afternoon when we finished our three hours of verbal jousting. Both the Judge and I were exhausted and retired to our respective hotels.

The next morning I awoke early to several knocks on my door. I opened it in my nightshirt. Five men, my council of advisors, walked solemnly into my room. To the original three, we had added Norman Judd, an anti-Nebraska Democrat who had become a Republican, and Gustave Koerner, lieutenant governor of Illinois and a German-American Republican leader from Belleville. We all drew up chairs in the sitting room.

Davis began, "Lincoln, Douglas made good on his promise to make hash of you yesterday."

"I know, I know," I said, shaking my head.

"You were on your heels the whole time," Davis continued.

"And why didn't you answer Douglas's questions?" asked Billy. "How could the crowd not have thought you were running away from him?"

Swett added, "I don't think it was wise to quote from your Peoria speech."

There was a brutal silence.

Judd broke it by saying, "It's simple. There are two alternatives. More of the same in Freeport next week, or a new strategy."

Davis replied, "Yes, Judd. We all know that."

"I have an idea," counseled Swett. "Douglas posed several questions for Lincoln and badgered him for not answering them. I suggest that Lincoln return the favor."

"Good idea, Swett," responded Davis.

"We could try to back him into a corner on his response to the Dred Scott decision," said Swett.

"Lincoln, you could ask him whether the people of a territory can, by lawful means, exclude slavery from their limits prior to the formation of a state constitution," added Judd.

"Yes, that's it!" agreed Davis. "He tries to weasel his way around Dred Scott with his patter about police regulations."

Judd continued, "That sticks it to him. If he answers, 'Yes,' he will alienate the Buchanan wing of his party and his southern supporters. That answer is more palatable in Illinois and helps him in the senate race, but it will ruin him for national office. If he answers, 'No,' he will lose this election to you."

I thought to myself that I was glad to have these people on my side.

Six days later, we met again in Freeport for the second debate. Fifteen thousand people flooded the small town.

Judge Douglas entered Freeport the night before with a cannon booming from one of his train cars. It was named "Popular Sovereignty," and it heralded his arrival at each of the debate sites. He was greeted with a torchlight parade. I rode to the debate site on a wagon drawn by two horses.

At 2 p.m. we were introduced and ready to begin.

I spoke first.

Early in my first hour, I asked Judd's question, "*Can the people of a United States territory, in any lawful way, exclude slavery from its limits prior to the formation of a state constitution?*"

In his ninety minutes, the Judge replied without hesitation that the people of a territory could introduce or exclude slavery through local police regulations which could be enacted by the local legislature. He had made this statement in Illinois, but now he declared it in debates which were attracting national attention. Because of the violence in Kansas, his opposition to the Lecompton constitution, and his defiance of the Dred Scott decision, his support in the South was dwindling rapidly. The Democratic Party was splitting into factions that followed either Buchanan or Douglas. It was an opportunity for the Republican Party.

That night I met with my advisors at dinner in the hotel where we were staying. They agreed that my performance had improved. I held my own against Douglas's onslaughts. Swett, however, felt that in my rejoinder, I had not gone on the attack when I had the opportunity. I had not responded to Douglas's answer to my question, and Swett thought it was a mistake.

Located at the southern tip of the state, 400 miles south of Chicago, was Jonesboro, the site of the third debate on September 15. The town was small, the county was poor, and the interest was minimal, especially since the nearby state fair attracted a larger crowd.

Sitting out on the hotel porch the night before, I could observe and reflect upon the appearance of Donati's comet with its large feathery tail sweeping across the sky in the west. It radiated from a spot next to Arcturus, the bright red star in the girth of Bootes, the shepherd. Jutting out from the front of the feather were two pencil-thin lines which formed a second tail. It was highly unusual. For hundreds of years comets had been omens of things to come. I wondered what this one could herald.

In the third debate, Douglas continued to attack me as a Black Republican abolitionist. He also cited the "House Divided" speech, asking why the nation could not endure half slave and half free—to leave it as the Founders had placed it.

I responded that the Founders had not placed slavery as the Judge contended.

"I say, that Judge Douglas and his friends have changed the policy from the position in which our fathers originally placed it. I say, in the way our fathers originally left the slavery question, the institution was in the course of ultimate extinction. I say when this Government was first established, it was the policy of its founders to prohibit the spread of slavery into the new Territories of the United States, where it had not existed."

At breakfast the next morning, Davis rapped the table for silence, and focused on me.

"Lincoln, we all agree that you were more assertive yesterday. That's what we've been hoping to see."

"There is still one important thing," said Judd. "You cannot allow him to keep taunting you about being a Black Republican and an abolitionist. No one knows the voters of this state better than you. You cannot win this election if you keep defending the negro. You must make a strong statement on this at the next debate."

On September 18, the Judge and I met in Charleston for the fourth debate.

It was my turn to speak first.

Reluctantly, I took Judd's advice. He was right. From the state newspapers we learned the race was tightening. My heart was in it. I had to win this election.

I spoke first and answered Douglas's charges.

"I will say then that I am not, nor ever have been, in favor of bringing about in any way the social and political equality of the

white and black races, that I am not nor ever have been in favor of making voters or jurors of negroes, nor of qualifying them to hold office, nor to intermarry with white people; and I will say in addition to this that there is a physical difference between the white and black races which I believe will forever forbid the two races living together on terms of social and political equality."

I made this statement because I had to, but I knew I would regret it.

There was a break of almost three weeks between the debate in Charleston and the next one in Galesburg. I returned home to Springfield to catch up with Billy on our law cases and to rest.

On a crisp fall day, I walked to the office. We greeted each other and assumed our usual places on the sofa and the chair next to it. He looked over at me with an expression of concern rippling across his face.

"Lincoln," he said, looking up from his newspaper, "you will not believe what is in the *New York Herald* this morning."

"That's James Gordon Bennett, and he hates both Douglas and me. Read it!"

"The title of the article is 'Exhausted to the Dregs.' Here's what it says, 'The controversy in Illinois between Lincoln and Douglas in every style, in all its variations, has been drawn off by these two tremendous spouters to the very dregs. From Lincoln to Douglas, and from Douglas to Lincoln, their discussions have degenerated into the merest twaddle upon quibbles, "forgeries," falsehoods, recriminations of the most vulgar sort.'"

"I told you," I said. "Bennett is an old line Democrat. He can't stand me because of my views on slavery, and he has called Douglas a traitor for defying Buchanan on Lecompton.

"Well, if it's national news, it's not the kind we need," said Billy.

"Billy, half of New York is in the clutches of the South. Bennett is just their mouthpiece."

That afternoon, as I walked out into the prairie to the east of Springfield, I thought about the Bennett article. Unsettling as it might have been, I wondered if he wasn't right. Through the four debates, Douglas was trying desperately to undo me with falsehood and bluster. He knew I wasn't an abolitionist, but his strategy was to put me on the defensive with baseless charges. In defending myself, I'd been drawn down to his level. This was what Bennett's reporter meant by twaddle.

On October 7, at the fifth debate in Galesburg with a crowd of 15,000, I began to frame my defining statement on slavery.

"*I suppose that the real difference between Judge Douglas and his friends, and the Republicans on the contrary, is, that the Judge is not in favor of making any difference between slavery and liberty–and consequently every sentiment he utters discards the idea that there is any wrong in slavery.*

"Now, I confess myself as belonging to that class in the country who contemplate slavery as a moral, social, and political evil, having due regard for its actual existence amongst us and the difficulties of getting rid of it in any satisfactory way, and to all the Constitutional obligations which have been thrown about it; but, nevertheless, desire a policy that looks to the prevention of it as

a wrong, and looks hopefully to the time when as a wrong it may come to an end."

At the sixth debate at Quincy on October 13, I continued to emphasize this point.

Douglas was tired, and while he occasionally spoke with passion, the result was listless delivery, as if he were going through the motions. He said nothing new after the first debate. His face was bloated because he was drinking heavily. His voice was becoming hoarse again.

He was starting to look like a cornered rat. I sensed that while he was in decline, I was ascending. I was no longer in awe of him. I had the last debate to finish refining my ideas about slavery and to make a statement on it for myself, my party, and my country.

On October 15, two days after the Quincy debate, came the debate at Alton. On the night before the debate, Judge Douglas and I travelled down the Mississippi River to Alton on the steamboat *Louisiana*. We greeted each other civilly, but we had no extended conversation. He was joined by his wife, Adele, who had been with him for each of our appearances.

I could not sleep and walked out to the upper deck. Red and green running lights adorned the port and starboard sides of the boat. From her twin smokestacks she belched showers of sparks and streams of thick black smoke into the velvety darkness.

I leaned over the railing and alternately looked down at the river, or off to the side at an occasional light on the shore, or up at the stars. The night was clear and quiet but for the constant clockwise thrashing of the huge paddlewheel at the vessel's stern. It was the sound of water being slapped, pummeled, and then furiously flung backward into splash and foam. The noise was relentless, but in its regularity, if not its monotony, it was oddly comforting. My black cloak, resting casually over my shoulders, puffed out slightly as the steady movement of the ship merged with a light, early morning breeze.

I had never felt as fulfilled in my life as I did at this moment. That, however, was no guarantee I would win. I could hold my own with Douglas, but to what purpose? Everyone thought that like two horses, we were running neck and neck. That was thrilling, but what would I do if I lost again? I would not challenge Trumbull for his Senate seat. But for five votes in the legislature, I would be senator and not Trumbull. I was becoming an old man, and finally, my political career would be over. Everyone would desert me except Billy.

When the steamboat docked at Alton in the morning, the Judge and his entourage disembarked and walked to the Alton hotel. Following behind them, I veered to the left toward the Franklin House, where I would meet with my advisors. After a morning train ride, Molly and Bob would join us at the hotel.

In the hotel parlor, Davis, Billy, Swett, Judd, and Koerner had already gathered. We greeted each other warmly and discussed the strategy for the last debate. Midway through the meeting, I took out my harmonica and began to play "Oh! Susanna."

Davis was shocked, Judd was horrified, and Billy and Koerner started to laugh.

"Lincoln, whatever are you doing?" asked Swett.

"Well, my friends," I said, "when Douglas rolls into town he is greeted with brass bands, military parades, flocks of pretty girls, and a thundering cannon. The least we can do for me is a few choruses of 'Oh! Susanna.'"

Just as we finished our meeting, there was a light knock on the parlor door. Koerner rose and opened it slowly.

"Mrs. Lincoln, what a pleasure to see you, and you as well, young man."

Molly was wearing a stately green dress which showed her full figure to advantage. Koerner led her over to me, and we sat down together on the sofa. Bob, who was looking quite grown up, sat next to us in an armchair.

"Mrs. Lincoln, how elegant you look today," remarked Judd.

"Thank you, Mr. Judd," replied Molly. "If I am to be on the platform with Mrs. Douglas, I must look my best, but she is, of course, much younger than I am."

"Mrs. Douglas may have youth," said Davis, "but you have the inner beauty of refinement and allure." Then he asked, "Was the train crowded?"

"It certainly was," Molly responded, "and all the men were declaring themselves for Mr. Lincoln because of his performance in these debates. Horace White told me they've been on the front page in all the national newspapers."

"Now, Koerner," I said, "tell Mary what you think of our chances. She's been rather dispirited lately."

"Sehr gut," said Koerner. "Mr. Lincoln will be our next senator. He is the orator of the age. The Judge is in his cups."

A band played in the distance.

"Time for us to face the music," said Davis.

For mid-October in Illinois, the weather was unseasonably warm. If it had been bright sunshine, the warmth of Indian summer would have been welcomed, but it was overcast and gray with a threat of rain. The humidity hung low and close over the Mississippi River. A hint of expectation was in the air, but it was hard to tell if it foreshadowed the final debate between the two rivals or the arrival of an afternoon storm.

The debate was scheduled for half past one o'clock, and the crowd began to gather. Alton was a hub for rail and steamship transport; the trains were packed and two steamships arrived from St. Louis. A joint committee of Democrats and Republicans oversaw the construction of a speakers' platform to the south of the newly erected city hall, a three-story building with a large cupola.

Both the Judge and I ascended the stairs and looked out over the crowd of over 5,000 people. A few of them were seated on wooden chairs and benches, but most were sitting on hay bales that had been set up in the town square. From the platform we had a view of the river as it flowed majestically in the distance. I could see the Missouri mudflats on which, long ago, Shields and I were to have fought a duel with cavalry broadswords.

Henry Billings called the proceedings to order. After the introduction of the dignitaries, he reviewed the format for the crowd.

When Douglas rose to speak, I could tell he was exhausted. His voice was so hoarse he could not be heard past the first few rows. His partisans, however, were familiar with his arguments and cheered and applauded at appropriate intervals.

In his first hour he gave an elaborate explanation of why he had opposed the Lecompton constitution in Kansas.

Toward the end of his hour, summarizing his arguments in the debates, he spoke with fervor.

"I hold that the signers of the Declaration of Independence had no reference to negroes at all when they declared all men to be created equal. They did not mean the negro, nor the savage Indians, nor the Fejee Islanders, nor any other barbarous race. They were speaking of white men. They alluded to men of European birth and European descent–to white men, and to none others, when they declared that doctrine. I hold that this Government was established on the white basis. It was established by white men for the benefit of white men and their posterity forever, and should be administered by white men, and none others."

It was now my turn to speak. This would be my last presentation of the seven debates. After responding to most of his standard arguments, it was now my turn to state my case as I had developed it over the last two months.

"The real issue in this controversy–the one pressing upon every mind–is the sentiment on the part of one class that looks upon the institution of slavery as a wrong, and of another class that does not look upon it as a wrong."

I closed with these words.

"That is the real issue. That is the issue that will continue in this country when these poor tongues of Judge Douglas and myself shall be silent. It is the eternal struggle between these two principles–right and wrong–throughout the world. They are the

two principles that have stood face to face from the beginning of time; and will ever continue to struggle. The one is the common right of humanity and the other the divine right of kings. It is the same principle in whatever shape it develops itself. It is the same spirit that says, 'You work and toil and earn bread, and I'll eat it.' No matter in what shape it comes, whether from the mouth of a king who seeks to bestride the people of his own nation and live by the fruit of their labor, or from one race of men as an apology for enslaving another race, it is the same tyrannical principle."

In his thirty-minute rejoinder, Douglas made his final observation with this statement.

"*He says that he looks forward to a time when slavery shall be abolished every where. I look forward to a time when each State shall be allowed to do as it pleases. If it chooses to keep slavery forever, it is not my business, but its own; if it chooses to abolish slavery, it is its own business–not mine. I care more for the great principle of self-government, the right of the people to rule, than I do for all the niggers in Christendom."*

Tuesday, November 2, Election Day was cold and rainy. I worked a half day in the office, ate supper at home, and then camped out in the telegraph office. The results of the elections came in sporadically throughout the evening and into the late hours of the night.

Combined votes for Republican candidates for the Illinois House of Representatives and the Senate were slightly ahead of the Democrats' totals, but because the most recent apportionment favored the Democrats, they led in more of the legislative races. It looked as if Republicans would win the overall vote, but the Democrats would control the legislature. Once again, I had been defeated for a U.S. Senate seat from Illinois. Once again, we were so close, but not quite there.

Finally around midnight, I walked home. The streets were wet and muddy. My path had been worn hog-back and was slippery. My foot slipped from under me, knocking the other one out of the way, but I recovered myself and landed square. I said to myself, "It's a slip and not a fall."

The pain of losing once more was slow to ease. I trudged to the office. There were a few cases for which we had to prepare. Playing with the boys and walking through Springfield with Molly began to revive my spirits.

A few days later, I wrote in a letter to my friend Anson Henry, "I am glad I made the late race. It gave me a hearing on the great and durable question of the age, which I could have had in no other way; and though I now sink out of view, and shall be forgotten, I believe I have made some marks which will tell for the cause of civil liberty long after I am gone."

Part Three

Chapter 12

I Had the Taste for It in My Mouth

Since it was early March, the prairie grass still wore its winter coat of light brown. Off in the distance, set against the lighter hues of the tall, sweeping grasses, were the dark, gray-brown trunks and limbs of the oak trees. Standing majestically, they were awaiting longer days and warmer temperatures, when they would burst out into the yellow-green of their first foliage. An occasional white farmhouse or decaying wooden barn dotted the landscape.

Molly and I were traveling by train from Springfield to Bloomington for a birthday party that Sarah Davis was giving for David Davis on March 9, 1859. Billy and Mary Maxcy Herndon were also invited, but they were not sitting with us because Molly still didn't care for Billy. She thought he drank too much and was not a suitable partner for me. There was tension between them that I simply ignored.

We were looking forward to the party, which also included Leonard Swett and his wife, Laura; and Jesse Fell, who lived in Bloomington and whose wife, Hester, was visiting relatives in Cincinnati.

I looked away from the window and turned toward Molly. She was in a mellow mood, perhaps because she was freed from fussing at three bustling boys for two days.

"I have you all to myself for a brief spell!" she said.

"Yes, you do," I replied, "and I shall enjoy it as much as you."

She turned reflective and said, "These last years have been good ones for us."

"They have indeed. The boys are happy and healthy, you have been a boon companion, and thanks to you, we have a house that is twice its original size. We talked about the plans, and when I came home from the circuit, it was done!"

"And you have included me in your political life," she added.

"Which is now over," I said dryly.

"Mr. Lincoln, there is talk of your running for president."

"Molly, it's just talk. You know that as well as I."

She looked disappointed and angry.

"You have no interest in it?" she asked.

"Seward is the probable nominee. If they need to balance the ticket with someone from the West, they might consider me for vice-president."

"Do you think Douglas will run?"

"Of course, he ran in '52 and '56. Why wouldn't he try again?"

"Will he win this time?"

"I don't think so, but we'll see. There are so many possibilities in this presidential year that trying to predict what will happen is useless."

We arrived in Bloomington in the mid-afternoon. Billy, Mary, Molly, and I rode in a carriage to the inn where we would spend the night. At first, we relaxed in our luxurious rooms, and then Molly and I took a walk through downtown Bloomington. When we reached the McLean County Courthouse, I amused her with stories of cases I'd won and lost there.

I loved telling the story of the Englishman Baddeley from Bloomington to whom Stuart sent me for one of my first trials. Baddeley looked me over and dismissed me from the case, remarking that I looked like "a rustic on his first visit to the circus."

Sarah Davis's invitation specified that we were to wear evening dress for the party.

For men, that meant a long black coat with a black vest and bow tie, and for women it was evening gowns. Formal dress was normally for large receptions and balls, but Davis's birthday was a special occasion for the Davis family and their closest friends.

The Davises' house was spacious and attractively furnished. Davis, who was becoming a wealthy man, talked of building a mansion in Bloomington for his and Sarah's later years. For the moment, their lifestyle was certainly pleasant, if not elegant.

The birthday guests first gathered in the parlor. We were all there but for Sarah, who was in the kitchen supervising the cook and the help who would serve us throughout the evening. Our conversation was pleasantries and catching up. It may have been surprising, but politics was not one of the topics. Unless Davis raised the subject, we agreed not to say a word about it.

We were all comfortably engaged in the parlor when Sarah rang a delicate glass bell to signify that we were to move into the dining room for the birthday supper. Davis, of course, was at the head of the oval dining room table with Sarah at the opposite end. Molly sat on Davis's right with Leonard Swett on his left. I was seated on Sarah's right with Mary Herndon next to me on my right. Billy was on Sarah's left, with Laura Swett and Jesse Fell in between him and Molly.

We dined scrumptiously with the main course of duck. It was served with a delicious gravy, which we dabbed up with our freshly baked bread. I was never one for refined food and drink, but the Davises were such gracious hosts that I could not disappoint them by not partaking energetically. As the server passed from guest to guest, I took seconds of the duck and gravy.

After dessert, Davis tapped his wine glass with a knife handle, the universal sign that he wished to speak.

"Sarah and I are delighted to welcome you all to my birthday celebration. You are among our closest and dearest friends, and we are honored that you could join us tonight. Normally I would open the floor for lengthy and witty toasts in my honor, and while I would certainly enjoy that, we have gathered you for a different purpose.

"Our friend Lincoln has recently made a noble canvas, which, if unavailing in this state, has earned him a national reputation, and made him friends everywhere. There is talk in the newspapers in our state and in Indiana that Lincoln should run for president. I would like us to discuss this possibility tonight. If we do think it's viable, how should he and we proceed?"

There was complete silence. The ticks of the grandfather clock in the dining room were audible.

When it became embarrassing, I exclaimed, "Just think of such a Sucker as me as president."

I laughed heartily, and some of them joined in.

Silence reigned once more.

Jesse Fell, who was a lawyer and a newspaper man, jumped in and said, "I have just returned from a lengthy trip to the eastern states. I can tell you that everywhere I was asked, 'Who is this man Lincoln?' I told them, 'There are two giants in Illinois, a little one you know, and a big one you don't.'"

"That's our biggest problem," continued Fell. "I propose that Lincoln write a short biography of himself and that we send it to all the eastern newspapers."

"Fell, that's very kind of you," I said, "but let's be realistic. I've served one term in the House and lost two races for the Senate. My executive experience is being the senior partner in a two-man law firm. Seward and Chase have both served as governors and senators of their states. Everyone knows them. Scarcely anyone, outside of Illinois, knows me. Besides, it's a matter of justice to those who have carried this movement forward, in spite of fearful opposition and personal abuse. I am ambitious and would like to be president, but there is no such good luck in store for me, as the presidency of these United States."

"But," broke in Molly, "Seward has given two speeches, one in which he said, 'there is a higher law than the Constitution,' and one last year in which he said we face 'an irrepressible conflict.' Chase is perceived as an abolitionist and cannot win the election. Bates has the temperament, but he is a family man and will probably not run."

"Well spoken, Mrs Lincoln," observed Davis. "No less than I would have expected from a woman who was often Henry Clay's dinner partner."

"If we look at the particulars of the election," said Swett, "I think they favor the Republicans.

"Douglas may not win the nomination. Lincoln trapped him into upholding the Freeport doctrine in the second debate. He had to go on record with his weaseling around the Dred Scott decision. The Democrats in the Senate have deposed Douglas from his chairmanship of the Committee on Territories. They are splitting into factions: for or against Douglas."

"Yes," I said, "Douglas has gone South, making speeches and trying to redeem himself."

"And are all of you familiar with what he's saying in them?" asked Billy. "He's said that in all contests between the negro and the white man, he is for the white man, but that in all questions between the negro and the crocodile, he is for the negro."

"I've heard that," I replied, "and I've deduced that it is a proposition in proportion, not unlike what I found in Euclid. What he is actually saying is that as the negro is to the crocodile, so is the white man to the negro; and as the negro may rightfully treat the crocodile as a beast or reptile, so the white man may rightly treat the negro as a beast or reptile. Once again, the negro is an inhuman brute."

"A point well taken, Lincoln. I still see Douglas as our biggest threat," said Davis. Looking over at me, he continued, "You pulled some of his teeth in the debates, but he is not yet a toothless lion."

Jesse Fell said, "I've learned that Douglas has cooked up a new strategy. He will pursue the Democratic nomination at their convention in Charleston, but if he fails to win because he has lost southern support, he will come our way and compete for the Republican nomination. Horace Greeley continues to beat the drum for Douglas. He could be a formidable candidate. Our party might be receptive if he looks like a winner. That's the first law of politics."

"No one trusts Douglas anymore," said Molly passionately. "I don't think the Republicans would turn to him. There's too much bad blood."

"Once again, I think you are right, Mrs. Lincoln," responded Davis.

We took a brief break while coffee was being served. Davis offered cigars to the men and brandy to all the guests. Davis, Billy, and Jesse Fell lit their cigars from the dinner candles, and all the men except me served themselves the brandy. Davis gave himself a generous pour. At some dinner parties, the women withdrew to the parlor, but in this case all the wives were highly interested in the political discussion, and remained at the dining room table.

When we reconvened, Davis continued to lead the discussion.

"What recommends our friend, Lincoln, for the Republican nomination," he began, "is what he has done for our party here in Illinois. Our long-term Whigs could have been at the throats of the Democrats who have recently joined them as Republicans. Free soilers have made peace with the abolitionists in the north of the state. Immigrants, mostly Germans, have somehow reached accommodation with their enemies, the Know Nothings.

"How has this happened? Lincoln has crafted a morally based position on slavery that is moderate and practical. It is acceptable to all the factions of our party. It's a model for the Republican Party nationally, and it's a winner for the election."

Billy added, "I'd compare Lincoln's balancing act to Blondin's latest feat. Have you all heard what he has done?"

"I haven't," said Sarah Davis, and she was joined in this admission by most everyone else at the table.

"I have not heard of Blondin," said Swett. "Tell me who he is and what he's done."

Billy was animated as he shared his familiarity with Blondin.

"Blondin is a French acrobat who has performed dangerous exploits in Europe for the past decade. His specialty is walking across a canyon or a mountain passage on a tightrope. He's come to America for the first time, and this summer will try to cross Niagara Falls. He's been warming up for the past month, and a few days ago he walked part way, not just by himself, but with his agent on his back. There was an article about it in the *Journal* last week. I'm surprised none of you saw it.

"The piece de resistance in August will be walking across the tightrope with a stove in a wheelbarrow. Midway he will cook an omelet and let it down to the passengers on a cruise ship underneath him."

"How extraordinary," said Laura Swett. "I've never heard of such a thing."

"Neither have I," said Mary Herndon. "Why didn't you tell me about this?"

"I knew you'd be terrified for the poor fellow. I just thought of it a minute ago," replied her chagrined husband.

"But, William, this is absolutely brilliant," observed Davis. "If this Blondin moves an iota, one jot or tittle, to the left or the right, he crashes down into the void with his agent, his wheelbarrow, and his stove on top of him."

All the guests looked horrified and waited to hear Davis's point.

"Yes, William, your meaning is clear, and an excellent comparison it is. Do you all follow?"

Since no one did, there was silence.

"It's simple. Lincoln's position on slavery is sensibly in the middle of our muddle. It's a centrist position, and it befits the man we've all come to know. Suppose our friend, metaphorically of course, were to walk across the tightrope with all the nation's goods and achievements crammed into that wheelbarrow, and the security and safety of everyone's home depended on his guiding it successfully over the falls. As he was carefully feeling his way along and balancing his pole with all his most delicate skill over the thundering cataract, would you have shouted to him, 'STEP TO THE RIGHT,' or 'STEP TO THE LEFT,' or would you have stood there speechless, and held your breath and prayed to the Almighty to guide and help him safely through the trial."

At this point, Swett entered the conversation, saying, "Davis, this is all very interesting and amusing, with a good point as well, but shouldn't we get back to your original idea? What strategy should we adopt if we want Lincoln to become a candidate for president? What should he be doing? What can we do to support him? Can we have a plan before we leave here tonight?"

"Getting us back to the particulars as usual, Swett," said Davis. "What a good way for us to end this delightful evening. What do you suggest?"

Swett paused for a moment, placed his right thumb underneath his chin with the other fingers cupping the right side of his face, and balanced his elbow on the table. He took the time to think carefully before responding to Davis's invitation.

"As for Lincoln," began Swett, "I think he should follow Douglas everywhere he speaks, particularly in Ohio, Indiana, and Kentucky, and respond the next day. He should employ the same strategy he used before and after his Peoria speech. It will be like the debates, and Lincoln will continue to get the better of the arguments.

"As for the rest of us, we should use all our contacts to procure speaking opportunities for him in the East. Billy, you know Theodore Parker and Horace Greeley. Perhaps they can help us. Davis, you also have influential friends in the East."

"Where is the convention?" Billy asked.

"Chicago," replied Davis.

"That's convenient," returned Billy. "Who arranged that?"

"Judd," said Davis, almost spitting out the word. Even in our own camp there was tension between an old line Whig and a Johnny-come-lately Democrat. Davis could not forgive Judd for voting for Trumbull in the 1855 Senate election.

Billy continued with his idea. "Over the next few months this will all heat up. Going into the Chicago convention, we need to have Lincoln positioned as the Illinois 'favorite son' candidate. That means all the delegates from Illinois must be pledged to vote for him, at least on the first ballot. It will give Lincoln momentum coming to Chicago. That's our job: to lock up those delegates for him."

"I will speak wherever people want to listen," I said, "and I deeply appreciate your confidence in me. Remember, however, that I find this possibility premature and likely to evaporate."

Molly and I enjoyed our holiday in Bloomington, and in the late afternoon we boarded the train for Springfield. We talked about the encouragement my friends had given me at the dinner party. When dusk descended over the prairie, Molly leaned her head on her backrest and fell into a deep sleep.

I realized that a politician had to live most of his life behind a mask. I feigned indifference to becoming president, but what were my true thoughts?

I believed there was so little likelihood of it happening that putting myself in the president's shoes was foolhardy. I was right when I said, "Just think of such a Sucker as me as president." If political experience and high office were prerequisites, I was severely wanting. How could I be fit for such a challenge?

There were several candidates in the Republican Party who had those qualifications. And what if I should vault over them and become president? Would they support me for the sake of the country and the party when they disagreed with me? Wouldn't they be expecting me to fail? They'd probably be plotting to succeed me in the next election. Would I become one of Shakespeare's tragic figures, spending all my time trying to foil their plots?

And then I considered the two previous occupants of the office.

Franklin Pierce was elected to the House from New Hampshire and then became a senator. He was a "dark horse" candidate in 1852 and won the election, but the job was too difficult for him, and he drank heavily while in office. Poor Pierce, he and his wife lost their eleven-year-old son in a train wreck two months before he was inaugurated.

Was being in high office beset with tragedy?

What about James Buchanan? No one had better experience for the presidency, and he had been inept.

But what if the sectional conflict should continue and worsen? What if the result were war?

Douglas was certain that, if he were elected, his presidency would be a time of transcontinental railroads and national expansion. He expected the Kansas-Nebraska Act to quell slavery agitation.

I was not as sanguine. I could foresee a time of conflict and war. Would I want to be president if that were to happen?

But finally, I considered the slavery issue. The position I had developed over a decade was one that I believed could diminish the problem. Slavery must be contained and allowed to die. We would reinstitute the Missouri Compromise. It would take years, but if that became the policy of the Republican Party and then the policy of the nation, I could see myself as president in 1860.

The truth was I had the taste for it in my mouth.

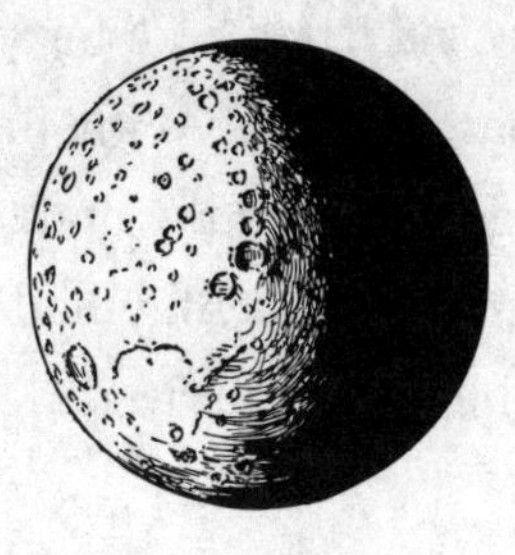

Chapter 13

By the Light of the Moon

"Lincoln, there's a letter here for you from someone who can barely write. With that scrawl, I don't know how it could get through the mail, but here it is."

We were in our office, and Billy had been through the morning mail by the time I arrived. He handed me the peculiar letter.

I tore it open and began to read it aloud.

Dear Abe,

It is my misfortune to tell you that Jack died last month. He was sick starting last year, but he went pretty fast this October. He always talked about how well you done. I ain't the same since he passed.

When you was in Salem, do you remember how you took a shine to Duffy and danced him on your knee? Duffy needs you now. He is charged with murder. He hit Pres Metzker but they say he was using a slung shot. Duffy says it was just his fist and that Norris hit him with the neck yoke. Metzger was full of liquor and fell off his horse two times before he come home. Norris is convicted and sent to jail for eight years.

I'm deathly afeard Duffy will go to the gallows. He is a good boy and has been in some scrapes, but none like this. Abe, I most probably can't afford your fees, but could you help an old friend?

Write to me so I know what to do.

Sincerely,

Hannah Armstrong

"Is this from someone you knew in New Salem?" asked Billy.

"Yes," I replied, "it's clear Hannah needs my help. I must leave for Petersburg this afternoon."

"How long will you be gone?"

"Well, if there's a trial, it will be several days."

"You should be fine," Billy said. "Things on the political front are oddly quiet."

The defendant, Duff Armstrong, sat with me in front of the judge and jury at the courtroom in Beardstown. He was tight-lipped, with an expression that swung like a pendulum between being anxious and being alarmed. Behind our table sat his mother, Hannah, who wore a sun bonnet on this warm May afternoon. A pretty young woman, the wife of the deceased James Preston Metzger, sat close to the lawyers for the state; she looked as if she was holding back tears. The room was full of spectators who were drawn to the entertainment of a murder trial.

Shades of brown, gray, and black created a subdued mood in the courtroom. The floor, the walls, and the ceiling were all formed from the dark and heavy oak that grew plentifully near Beardstown. Perhaps the crowd had chosen muted, darker clothing because they apprehended the possible result of the day's proceedings.

I slumped back in my chair, extended my legs, and stared at the ceiling. I was simply observing the pattern in the grain of the wood above me.

Judge Harriot addressed me as the attorney for the defense of William Duff Armstrong.

"Cross examination, Mr. Lincoln?"

"Yes, your honor," I replied. I rose slowly and approached the witness stand.

In the chair to the right of the judge on the raised platform sat a young man about the same age as Duff Armstrong. He was dressed plainly in a gray-green denim shirt, dark blue overalls, and worn boots. He had a pleasant face and seemed relaxed and confident.

"Mr. Allen," I asked, "what brought you to Walker's Grove last August?"

"The religious meeting, sir."

"You came to hear Rev. Cartwright?"

"No, sir," the young man blushed, "cain't say we did."

"And who, Mr. Allen, is we?"

"My friends, sir, we come to have a good time."

"And a good time consists of . . .?"

"Horse racing, betting . . ."

" . . . and drinking spirits?"

"Yes, sir."

"Mr. Allen," I continued, "do you know the defendant?"

"He ain't a close friend, sir."

"But you know him."

"Yes, sir."

"Were you friends with Jamie Norris and Pres Metzker?"

"Yes, sir."

"Mr. Allen, you gave us the particulars this morning, but will you briefly recount the events that led to the injuries Pres Metzker sustained last August 29."

"Yes, sir. The meeting was finishing up the next day, so we was all havin' one last go-round. The boys was drinking all day."

"But you were not," I interposed.

"No, sir, not near as much as them. Anyway, Duffy and Jamie was riled at Pres 'cause he'd messed with them. I seen the brawl where Pres worked Duffy over pretty good, but they had a drink afterwards. I guess Duffy was still hot about it. Anyway, it was pretty late, and I seen Duffy and Pres take two more drinks and then walk t'ward the trees. They was in the clearing and Jamie had a stick of wood and Duffy had his slung shot. They was pretty open about it, and I could see pretty clear."

"What time was it?"

"About 11, sir."

"How did you know that?"

"The wagon sellers cut off the liquor at 11 o'clock, sir."

"How were you able to see so clearly?"

"From the campfires and the moon."

"From the moon?"

"Yes, it was bright and shined above the trees."

"What phase was it?"

"Three quarters, sir."

"Where was Metzker at this point?"

"He was makin' t'ward that grove of trees. He looked pretty shaky."

"How far away from them were you?"

"About a hundred feet, sir."

"And could you see through the trees?"

"Yes, sir, there was no clouds, the fires was near the whiskey wagon, and the moon shined through them."

"Where was the moon positioned?"

"I'd say overhead—where the sun is at noontime or maybe at 1 o'clock during the day."

"And by moonlight you saw Jamie Norris hit Pres Metzker in the back of the head with a thick wooden stick?"

"Yes, sir."

"And by moonlight you saw Duff Armstrong strike Pres Metzker near the right eye with a slung shot?"

"Yes, sir."

"Will you show the jury how you saw Duff Armstrong deliver this blow?"

"Yes, sir."

The young man rose from the witness stand, reached toward his pocket, arched his right arm overhead, and struck downward—the motion a man might make with his extended arm when chopping with an axe.

"And this you saw by the light of the moon?"

"Yes, sir."

"And what time was this, Mr. Allen?"

"Just after 11 o'clock, sir."

I walked slowly back over to the table and pawed through my tattered briefcase. Adjusting my spectacles, I rustled through the papers. I was in no hurry; a sense of quiet expectation settled over the courtroom.

"Here it is," I said quietly to myself.

I drew out a ratty, dog-eared booklet and presented it to the judge.

"Judge Harriot, this is a *Jayne's Almanac* for the year 1857. Will you please open it to the page for August 29?"

After some initial fumbling, Judge Harriot leafed through the booklet and announced he had found the requested page.

"Your honor, if you will run your finger down the page, you will find the time the moon set on the evening of August 29-30. Your honor, will you please read the entry from the almanac?"

Judge Harriot looked uncertain, but he did as I requested and seemed more at ease once he had found the requested fact.

"Just after midnight, at 12:03 a.m.," he replied.

"Your honor, members of the jury," rose my voice, "the moon set at 12:03 a.m. on the night of August 29-30. It was not overhead. At 11 o'clock that night it would have been just above the horizon. What little light it provided would never have illuminated the scene that Mr. Allen has so clearly depicted for us."

A wave of laughter erupted in the courtroom. The chief witness for the prosecution looked out over the crowd. He looked as if he'd been struck by lightning. The laughter died down, and I told the judge I had no further questions for the witness. It was now time for the closing arguments.

After Hugh Fullerton delivered the prosecution's closing statement, Judge Harriot nodded toward the defense table and asked, "Mr. Lincoln, I presume you will be presenting for the defense?"

I replied, "I will, your honor."

I rose deliberately from my chair and removed my white linen suit coat. I dropped it carelessly over the chair. Next I removed my vest and black cravat, revealing a pair of homespun suspenders.

I turned toward the jury and began, "My friends, you have a solemn assignment before you on this fine spring afternoon. You are charged with determining whether William Duff Armstrong and James Norris acted in concert in the killing of James Preston Metzger."

I clasped my hands behind me and thrust my head forward.

"Now, this morning you heard from the defendant's friends. Yes, they are his friends, and it is our friends who know us best. They told us that Duff did no murder; that he could do no murder; that he did not take a life; that he could not take a life."

"You heard that the boys reckoned they might get up to some high jinx, that they came to the camp to roister 'mong themselves those summer nights, but Duff's not the kind of boy who'd turn on a friend and beat him—to death.

"His friends told us about his unblemished character. No charge of any kind is recorded against him. He's the worthy son of a widowed mother."

As I warmed to my task, I unclasped my hands and interlocked them into a supportive web. I grasped one thumb with the other. My voice eased into a more melodious pace.

"Now let's look at what happened and what didn't happen at 11 p.m. on August 29.

"Mr. Allen testified that he saw Norris strike Metzker from behind with a stick of wood, most likely a neck yoke, and that Armstrong hit Metzker from the front with a slung shot.

"Mr. Allen is the only witness who says he saw Armstrong and Norris together at 11 p.m. in the glade with what he tells us were the murder weapons. He says he saw this by the light of the moon.

"Nel Watkins testified that he is the owner of the slung shot, and that it was in his possession on the night of August 29. His testimony confirms the defendant's statement that he never hit Pres Metzker with a slung shot. Nel Watkins went to sleep before 11 that night, and he put the slung shot under a blanket on the wagon seat before retiring. Watkins told us that on the following day it must have fallen to the ground near the scene of the crime.

Armstrong says he hit Metzker hard in the face when they fought that afternoon, but after the fight they patched it up with a shot of whiskey.

"The only person who tells us that Armstrong and Norris acted in concert to give Metzker the fatal blows that night is Charlie Allen. And remember, he saw this by the light of the moon.

"Both doctors testified that Metzker sustained two wounds to the skull, one in the front above the right eye and the other in the left rear.

"Doc Parker told us that the blow to the back of the head, the one that Norris inflicted on Metzker, probably caused the frontal contusion above Metzker's right eye. That's the same place that Armstrong says he struck Metzker with his fist earlier in the day.

"Doc Parker says the wound above the eye was superficial. He says it was not made with a weapon. He expected it to heal on its own.

"When Doc Parker examined Metzker, Pres told him he'd fallen from his horse twice on the way home. Doc surmised he was still under the influence. He died three days later.

"Metzker himself believed he was ill from the liquor and the falls from his horse.

"Charlie Allen tells us that Armstrong and Norris acted in concert to harm Metzker; Charlie Allen tells us that Duff Armstrong struck Pres Metzker above the right eye with a slungshot; Charlie Allen accuses Duff Armstrong of manslaughter.

"And Charlie Allen saw all this by the light of the moon.

"The prosecution's case rests on the testimony of Charles Allen. I am not calling Charlie Allen a liar, but as a witness in this trial giving a crucial piece of evidence, his memory has failed him. He has misrepresented himself. He has not done this purposely, but how can we accept the rest of his testimony when one piece of it is fatally flawed?

"Can you trust his testimony? Are you willing to send a young man to prison, to take him away from his widowed mother, on the word of someone who has not told the truth?

"The clear and simple truth is that Duff Armstrong is innocent. He did not attack Pres Metzker. Pres Metzker died from his own doing. He was injured by Norris's blow, but his drunken falls from his horse caused his death. He knew this himself.

"You need to restore Duff to his widowed mother. He is a good young man who was raised right by his parents.

Duff knows his Commandments. Thou shalt do no murder. He has done no murder.

"When I first came to Salem in the summer of 1831, the summer after the winter of the Deep Snow, I was a piece of floating driftwood. I was penniless. I had no friends. I was alone. Denton Offutt had hired me to be a clerk in his store. I knew nothing of the world, and I was nothing to the world.

"When I had been in Salem a month, Offutt wagered that I could lick any man in town. He hadn't reckoned on the Clary's Grove boys. Chief among them was Jack Armstrong.

"Jack and I wrestled each other to a draw. It was my real welcome to Salem. From then on Jack was my friend. When I was elected captain of our company in the Black Hawk War, I chose Jack to be my first sergeant. When I first ran for the legislature, Jack and the Clary's Grove boys rounded up votes for me.

"Jack and Hannah took me into their home and fed me. Hannah fixed my torn pants and knitted shirts for me.

"For I was hungry, and ye gave me meat; I was thirsty, and ye gave me drink; I was a stranger and ye took me in; Naked and ye clothed me . . ."

"Then Hannah gave birth to another boy, and Hannah and Jack named him William Duff Armstrong. He grew to be strong and healthy. I rocked his cradle when he was a baby, and when he grew older, I bounced him on my knee.

"When I got settled at the Rutledges', I stopped by to see Hannah and Jack and to visit with Duffy. 'U'cle Abe,' he would call me. You know, I've never liked that name, but it sounded fine coming from that little boy.

"I have known this boy and his family since my years in Salem.

"His father died just after Duff was arraigned last fall. He'd been sick, but he wanted to see his boy's name cleared.

"I am here to do that for Jack and Hannah.

"My path took me away from Salem, and the town winked out shortly after I left. Jack and Hannah moved to Petersburg to buy a farm. Jack was a farmer all his life. He and Hannah raised their four boys to be good boys and to obey the law. The boys took after their father.

"In my work, I have met people across Illinois from all walks of life. None of them compares with Jack Armstrong. He was a simple, honest, loyal, and good man.

"My own boys will have opportunities that Jack never knew; as they grow up, I want them to be just like him.

"Duff is his father's son. He is also his mother's son. From Jack he learned to work hard and enjoy life. From Hannah he learned to be kind and generous.

"Duff is not a murderer. Duff did not act in concert with Jamie Norris to take Pres Metzker's life.

"I hope you will make Duff Armstrong a free man before sundown."

The jury returned a verdict in 45 minutes. They found William Duff Armstrong not guilty.

Hannah was not in the courtroom when the jury deliberated. She had returned to her room at the Farmer's Home Hotel in Beardstown. She preferred the privacy of her room for the moment when she would learn her son's fate.

I was in the town square when Milton Logan, a farmer from Beardstown, handed up the verdict.

The news of Duff's acquittal spread quickly through the town. Janey Cole, a friend of Hannah's from Petersburg, rushed to the hotel with the news.

Within minutes of the verdict, Hannah and I had returned to the courtroom. It was a scene of jubilation.

In her wrinkled calico dress, which was now wet from tears and perspiration, and with her sun-bonnet still in place, Hannah hugged me. I towered over her as her head rested on my chest. Tears streamed from her eyes and from mine.

She could barely speak. "Abe," she gasped, "I can never repay you for what you have done."

"Hannah," I whispered, "Hannah, I'll hear no more of it. Your joy for your son is my payment."

After I spoke with Hannah, I turned to Duff and motioned to him to step outside for a private conversation.

Duff looked apprehensively into my eyes.

"Uncle Abe?" Duff's voice quavered.

I put my hand on Duff's shoulder.

"Young man, let this be a lesson. You were fortunate. At times you have been wayward and dissolute. You have dishonored yourself under the influence of liquor. Be a credit to the name of your father and a comfort to your mother."

Duff was nearly speechless, but he stammered out, "I . . . will . . . Uncle Abraham."

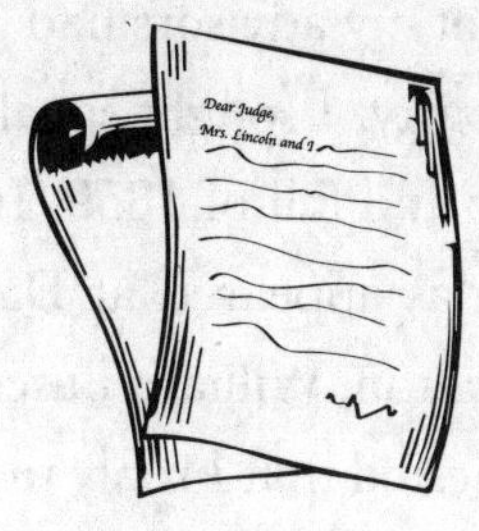

Chapter 14

Men Who Came West to Better Themselves

I took the advice that my advisors had given me at Judge Davis's birthday party. I sought speaking engagements through the summer and fall of 1859. In Ohio, I spoke a few days after Douglas appeared at Dayton, Cincinnati, Columbus, and Hamilton. William Bascom, a Republican official in Ohio, requested that I reply to Douglas because, "We desire to head off the little gentleman." I countered his arguments for popular sovereignty much as I had in the debates.

In Pennsylvania, Indiana, Iowa, and Minnesota, I spoke at the behest of Republican leaders in those states. On the slavery question, I tried to steer a middle course between popular sovereignty and abolition. We looked to the results of the fall elections in those states for a clue to whether the Republican message of moderation was resonating with the voters.

When the voters did decide in mid-October, the returns were heartening. Republicans won clear victories in all five states. We put Douglas and the Democrats back on their heels.

This was more evidence that, if the Republicans stayed together, we could win the presidential election in 1860.

Around election day, Molly received a letter from Julia Trumbull in Washington. She wrote that after giving birth to a daughter, Adele Douglas contracted a debilitating fever. Her condition worsened, and several days later the doctors feared for her life. The Judge cancelled all his public appearances to be at his wife's bedside. At the time of Julia's letter, it remained an extreme illness.

For a number of reasons, I found it hard to sleep that night. I rose from my bed and sat down at the little desk. In one of the cubbyholes was the text of a speech I was writing in response to a long article Judge Douglas wrote in *Harper's Magazine* on popular sovereignty. I took out my draft and read my last sentence. I was tired of Douglas's claim that local legislation could thwart the Dred Scott decision, and wrote, "I suppose the institution of slavery really looks small to him. He is so put up by nature that a lash upon his back would hurt him, but a lash upon anybody else's does not."

I paused to look out the window and saw the gas light atop the lamppost. It flickered in the light breeze. In a brief moment of reflection, I thought, "Here I am savaging a man who is about to lose his wife, and perhaps another child. We are no longer friends, but we are still linked as men who came west to better ourselves. We were both successful, but now we contend for one final step."

How could I ignore such tragic news?

I opened the top drawer and found the letter paper.

October 17, 1859

Dear Judge,

Mrs. Lincoln and I are distressed to learn that Mrs. Douglas is extremely ill after having given birth to your daughter.

Political conflict has altered our relations, but that does not prevent Mrs. Lincoln and me from praying for Mrs. Douglas's recovery and for baby Ellen.

Remembering the days when we were friendly rivals, Mrs. Lincoln and I send cordial greetings to you and your family.

Sincerely,

A. Lincoln

The following morning, when I walked into the office, I found Billy in an extreme state of agitation. I had never seen him like this.

"Billy, whatever has happened?" I asked.

"Lincoln, it's earthshaking. It will set the two sections of the country at each other's throats."

"Whatever can it be."

Billy picked up our copy of the *New York Daily Tribune* and read to me.

"A most extraordinary telegraphic bulletin startled the whole country yesterday—one importing that an insurrection had just broken out at Harpers Ferry, Virginia, and that it was the work of negroes and Abolitionists! That some sort of disturbance has taken place in that locality is manifest; for it seems that the telegraphic wires are broken at that point, and the running of the trains of the Baltimore and Ohio Railroad interrupted."

Over the next few days, we learned what had happened and the effect it was having on the country.

John Brown was the leader of the Pottawotomie Massacre in Kansas where he and his sons murdered five pro-slavery settlers. In the summer of 1859, Brown and several of his followers rented a farm on the Maryland side of Harper's Ferry, Virginia, where a federal armory and arsenal were located.

Brown's goal was to capture the federal buildings in Harpers Ferry and to launch a slave revolt that would ultimately include the slaves of the deep South. He and his men amassed a stockpile of rifles at the farmhouse.

On the evening of October 16 and under the cover of darkness, he began the revolt. Brown, two of his sons, and sixteen other men, five of whom were negroes, crept into Harpers Ferry and quickly took possession of the bridges leading into the town and the armory and arsenal. In the arsenal were 100,000 rifles. The raiders killed a negro watchman who was investigating a train delay at one of the bridges. The shots woke the town, and calls went out for the militia.

On the 17th, over the course of the day, the militia and townspeople skirmished with Brown and his men. By 3 p.m., they forced the insurrectionists who were left into the armory's firehouse. At 11 p.m., ninety Marines arrived at Harpers Ferry under the leadership of Col. Robert E. Lee and Lieutenant J. E. B. Stuart.

In the morning, the Marines crushed the rebellion and captured John Brown. He had lost his two sons and eight other men.

When Billy and I had the full report, we discussed the country's response. Since Brown was trying to incite a slave revolt, he was reviled in the South. Many southerners blamed Brown's raid on the Black Republican abolitionist party. Southern leaders saw this as a time to take their destiny into their own hands. A southern newspaper account reported, "The Harpers Ferry invasion has advanced the cause of disunion more than any other event that has happened since the formation of the Government." In the North, John Brown soon became a hero since he'd had the courage to act on his convictions. Although his raid failed, the Harpers Ferry Revolt demonstrated the violence some abolitionists saw as the only way to end slavery.

"This is grim, Billy, very grim," I said to him. "Our sectional conflict has entered a new phase. The southerners will start to arm themselves against more uprisings. They fear us, and they fear their slaves. They fear we will fight to free their slaves."

"This could mean civil war," Billy added. "I've seen editorials in some of the southern newspapers that say they should leave the Union if a Republican is elected president."

"Well, I think it depends on which Republican."

When I left the office in the late afternoon, I walked down Eighth Street toward our house. Willie and Tad didn't know when I would return, but they knew this was my most likely route. Sure enough, they were waiting for me. I pulled Tad up on my shoulders and took Willie's hand the rest of the way.

"Papa," piped up Tad, "can we wrestle with you on the carpet when we get home"

"Of course, my boys, but it depends on how your mother is feeling."

"She went to visit Aunt Elizabeth and isn't home yet," said Willie.

"That's good news for us, but we'll have to be on the lookout for her."

Tad asked, "Papa, can we come to the office with you on Sundays when Mama is at church?"

"I'm afraid not," I replied. "Mr. Herndon hasn't forgiven you for pulling the books off the shelves, bending his pen points, and rolling his inkwell across his desk."

We arrived home and commenced the wrestling. It was one of our favorite activities, but Molly thought it was beneath me. We did it anyway and were careful to listen for her coming up the steps. When she did, the boys shot outside, and I jumped into my chair by the fireplace.

She arrived and greeted me warmly and then said, "You were wrestling with them again."

"How can you tell?" I laughed.

"You need to do a better job of straightening your hair, and your shirt is cattywampus."

"You are the one person I can't fool," I laughed again.

Molly said, "Two letters came for you today. I think one is from Douglas and the other is from New York."

She rose, walked toward the kitchen, and then returned with the letters.

"Yes, this one is definitely from Douglas. Could you tell by the handwriting?" I asked.

"It's very distinctive," she observed.

I opened the letter and read it to her.

November 1, 1859

Dear Lincoln,

Thank you for your kind words.

Mrs. Douglas has improved and the baby survives. The doctor tells us the danger has passed.

I regret as well that our relations have altered.

Please come visit me in the White House where we can sit by the fire on a winter afternoon and remember earlier times.

Sincerely,

S. A. Douglas

Neither of us spoke. Molly gave me the second letter.

I opened it, and read it twice to myself. Then I rose from my chair and paced back and forth in the parlor.

"Husband, what can this mean?"

I read her the text of the letter.

Hon. A. Lincoln.

will you speak in Mr. Beechers church Brooklyn on or about the twenty ninth (29)

November on any subject you please pay two hundred (200) dollars.

Jas. A. Briggs

"Molly, this is what we've been hoping for—it's an invitation to lecture in New York! Thomas Corwin, the senator from Ohio and one of the finest orators in the country, will speak next month. I can't be ready for November 29, so I'll have to ask for a later date, maybe in January or February."

"Is Beecher the brother of Harriet Beecher Stowe?"

"Yes, and one of the leading clergymen in the East in his own right," I said.

"Important people will be there. You will have to prepare even more than usual."

"That's what is so grand about this. Davis will be here later this week. I'll talk it over with him and Billy."

That night I could not sleep. The speech in New York was an opportunity. If I took advantage of it, I could gain national recognition. It would advance my chance to become the Republican nominee for president.

This raised two questions: was I fit to be president and did I want to be president?

I had been hiding behind the mask of believing and saying there was no chance it could happen. Far more qualified men than I had failed to win the presidency, Henry Clay among them. Certainly there was no one more qualified than he.

It would take a miracle for me to win the nomination. But what if that miracle were to occur? I could imagine the circumstances that might lead to it, but several key pieces had to fall in place. Again, the odds were minimal.

As for being fit, didn't each man who became president wrestle with that as he approached his nomination? The most important quality for being president was to learn and grow in the office. I'd done that all my life.

I understood politics. My eight years in the state legislature was my apprenticeship. My twenty years on the law circuit introduced me to all the problems and personalities common to humanity. Building the Republican Party in Illinois gave me the chance to apply all the principles I had learned as a lawyer and politician at the state level. Washington was all this on a grander scale.

Did I want to be president?

It was every politician's dream. From the thousands in eighty years of our country's history had emerged 15 men. Would I become the 16th? Not likely, but not impossible.

I knew one thing. To pursue the office, I must have the self-confidence and the self-reliance to know that I could serve my country as president.

The outlook for the next presidency was grim. Was I the person to lead the country through the difficult times ahead? I believed I could be.

Three days later, Billy and Davis met with me in our office.

"Lincoln, this is splendid news that you will speak in Beecher's church," Davis whooped delightedly. "I am told it will be a distinguished audience. Have you chosen a topic?"

"Friends, before we get into that, there are some particulars I should mention to both of you.

"The original invitation was for the 29th of November, but we have agreed to delay it until February 27. That gives me more time to prepare. Next is that I am to be paid a fee of $200. That is the largest amount I have ever made from a speech. It will help pay for the addition to our house. That alone is impetus enough for me to accept the invitation.

"The next thing I have learned is that it's a lecture. That leads me to deduce what it isn't. It isn't a campaign appearance or another Lincoln-Douglas debate without the Judge attending or a closing statement at a trial. It is more formal, and that causes me to caution anyone who will be looking for rhetorical flourishes. It may strike you as a bit dry, but I have something in mind that will highlight the skills I have learned in court and my study of Euclid.

"The speech will have three parts. I have already written some of it.

"For the first part of my lecture, I will report on research I will conduct into the 39 signers of the Constitution—everyone from Rufus King and Roger Sherman to George Washington. I believe that through this research I can demonstrate that a majority of the Founders opposed the extension of slavery. In the second part, I will address a few words to the Southern people. I will confront them on the dangers of sectional conflict, and on their responsibility for breaking up the Union, if that should occur. Finally, I will speak a few words to our fellow Republicans. Though provoked, we cannot respond with passion and ill-temper. We must do what we can to ensure that all parts of our country are at peace and in harmony with each other. This is no easy task since we need to let the South alone, but also to act on the principle that slavery is wrong."

"Lincoln," said Davis, "this speech could make you a national leader. They expect you to be a frontier hayseed, and they will get a statesman. It may be your breakthrough. Let us hope so."

Billy added, "There is speculation that Briggs invited you because he is a Chase man and hopes you will cut into Seward's support."

"That could happen," observed Davis, "but if we deadlock, Douglas is still ready to turn on the Democrats and become a Republican."

"It is ironic," I replied, "that Douglas can do that because of Lecompton, where for once he showed himself to be a man of principle. He alienated Buchanan and the southern Democrats, but made himself acceptable to Horace Greeley, who is still pushing the idea of running him as a Republican."

"It is also ironic," said Billy, "that you may have done yourself in for senator by trapping him in the Freeport Doctrine, but at the same time opened the door to the presidency. Did you think of that at the time?"

"No," I said definitively.

"Sometimes the serendipitous prevails in politics, but enough of all this for the moment," declared Davis.

He added, "Lincoln, as your friend and campaign manager, I am going to give you a piece of advice. We all need a diversion once in a while. Clear your head, and come with me for a brief visit. There is a production of *Hamlet* performed by a British company that is touring America and playing in Bloomington tomorrow night. It is the entire play, which is rare out here in the provinces. You and Mary can stay with us and take the train back to Springfield the next day. I know Shakespeare is not Mrs. Lincoln's favorite entertainment, but she and Sarah can enjoy each other's company, while we sneak off to the theater."

That night I had another strange dream.

It began in a castle near the sea. I was in the king's court, but betrayed by friends, and exiled from the country. Imprisoned on a ship, I had no idea where I was being taken.

On the second day, we encountered a frightful storm. At its height, another ship with broken masts rocked toward us on the angry waves. On it was a cargo of black men. Our captain gave the order to rescue as many of them as we could.

There were almost one hundred left.

I offered to give up my place and board the ship with the black men. The captain accepted gleefully.

Fortunately that night the storm passed and sea became calm. Three days later, we floated to the shore. The next morning, when I awoke, the others had disappeared.

I discovered that we had landed in my own country. I was alone and free.

Chapter 15

This Was a Test I Had to Pass

After Davis and I attended the performance of *Hamlet*, we returned to his house. Molly and Sarah had retired for the evening. We sat together by the fire in Davis's study, where he was smoking a cigar and drinking a glass of brandy. I was deep in thought and stared intently at the fire.

Davis asked, "What do you make of it?"

I continued to look into the fire, sighed deeply, and then said, "Hamlet is surrounded by a web of overwhelming evil. He has no one he can trust, not even his friend Horatio. Amidst this evil and treachery, he must ferret out the truth."

"I'd have more sympathy for him if he weren't such a ditherer," replied the judge.

"I think it's much more complicated than that."

Davis looked puzzled.

"The state of Denmark is 'rotten' at the beginning of the play. At the end Fortinbras will become ruler of a restored Denmark.

"What has caused Denmark to be restored?" I asked.

"The death of the king and all those who allied themselves with him. Claudius's final treachery backfires on him."

"That's right, but for one thing."

"And what is that?"

"Denmark has been restored by Hamlet's sacrifice of his own life. It is only Hamlet's blood that can redeem Denmark. The entire play is his growing understanding of that."

"But what about his delaying?"

"Hamlet must grow into the man who can sacrifice his life at the end. At the beginning he is a callow undergraduate, though perhaps an older one. He is hopelessly immature, caught in circumstances that would overwhelm the most poised young man. Yes, there are moments of indecision, and in his soliloquies, when we hear from his soul, he reveals his deep despair."

"Go ahead," said Davis, who still looked dubious.

"The Hamlet of acts four and five is very different from the earlier Hamlet. He makes peace with himself, his essential goodness shines through, and he begins to accept the sacrifice he will have to make to cleanse Denmark of its 'rottenness.'

"At the end of act one, he says, 'The time is out of joint. O, cursed spite, that ever I was born to set it right.' He has to accept what fate has decreed for him. He will be the person who redeems the time from the evil that cloaks it.

"Now, Davis, I will ask you, what is the most important line in the play?"

"Lincoln, it's impossible to answer that question."

"I can."

"Go ahead."

"No, I asked you the question. You are evading me."

"Oh, Lincoln, I am wracked with indecision."

"I am not. The most important line in the play is what Hamlet says to Horatio in act five just before the fencing match. He says, 'The readiness is all.'"

I added, "He has accepted his fate. It has taken him the entire play to get there."

"Lincoln, that's rather ingenious, but for all your delicious reasoning, I still think he's a Shakespearean tragic hero who fails to act and causes the state to collapse. He's lucky that Fortinbras is around to pick up the pieces."

"Perhaps we should submit it to a jury," I suggested.

"We should do that, and perhaps we'd get a surprise. Further instructions from the judge? A jury that couldn't make up its mind?"

I laughed and added another thought. "I've read it many times, and I've seen two productions of *Scenes from Hamlet*, but tonight I was struck by how utterly alone he is. I can't imagine being in his situation."

"Lincoln, it may be your fate to be in that situation. What if you are elected president of the United States?"

"There's very little evidence that will happen."

"But if you are elected, are you ready to be president?"

"I won't know until I get there."

"That's fair, but it's not a sufficient answer. Of course you will have doubts, but like Hamlet, you may have to accept your fate."

"And what might that be?"

"A situation worse than Hamlet's. Whoever is president must prepare to be utterly alone. You will have few friends, and even they might not be trustworthy. You will have colleagues, but they will always be after something or trying to influence you. Your wife has been helpful in Illinois, but she was over her head in Washington as the wife of an obscure congressman. It is a recipe for loneliness and keeping your own counsel. I wouldn't wish it on anyone.

You must be prepared for the most difficult presidency since Washington."

On the train home to Springfield, I reflected on my late-night conversation with Davis.

Because I viewed it as highly improbable that I should be elected president, I had not imagined myself in that role. I believed I was ready to be president, but as I told Davis, I would not know unless I were to win and serve in the office. With his extensive experience in Congress, that was not a concern for Douglas, and Seward had been a successful governor of New York as well as a noted senator—he too had no qualms about his readiness.

I decided I would continue to approach it step by step and see where the road took me. I wasn't dodging my own uncertainty, but it wasn't productive to dwell on it. I had always been motivated by a mysterious sense of purpose. It carried me through all my defeats and disappointments. It was best to let the events unfold.

The next step was the opportunity to speak at Henry Ward Beecher's church in Brooklyn before an illustrious audience. I had four months to prepare.

The framework of the speech was already in place. Now I had to write each of the sections. The first one was the hardest, and my objective was ambitious. I believed I could trace the voting records of the signers of the Constitution and find that a majority of them were against the expansion of slavery.

My quest began with the sources in the law library of the Capitol Building. The Annals of Congress and

Congressional Globe gave me access to some of the information I needed. Then came research in two basic sources: my own copy of Jonathan Elliot's *The Debates in the Several State Conventions on the Adoption of the Federal Constitution as Recommended by the General Constitution at Philadelphia, in 1787*, and the Lincoln-Herndon law firm's copy of James Kent's *Commentaries on the Constitution.*

From my study of these records and documents, I established that of the 39 signers of the Constitution, 21 were opposed to the expansion of slavery—a clear majority. This was the piece that allowed me to refute Douglas and popular sovereignty and to make my own argument for containing slavery.

Since the other two sections were based on statements I had made over the past six years, they flowed easily into the speech.

By early February, I had written a final draft. What came next was the extensive rehearsal after which I would feel comfortable delivering it. My goal was to memorize the text.

I did this by walking around our neighborhood with either Willie or Tad on my shoulders. One morning Willie and I encountered my friend Jesse Dubois outside his house. Jesse and his family had moved to Springfield in 1858 when he become state auditor. Our friendship dated back to our days in the Illinois legislature. He and his son Fred were raking the leaves in their front yard.

As we approached, I was reciting a paragraph from the first section of the speech.

"Is it not a little presumptuous in anyone at this day to affirm that the two things which that Congress deliberately framed, and carried to maturity at the same time, are absolutely inconsistent with each other?"

"Uncle Abe," asked Fred, "what does all that mean?"

Atop his ten-foot tower, Willie called down to Fred, "It has something to do with Stephen Douglas. Papa doesn't like him anymore."

"That's not quite true, William Wallace." I added, "It's a bit like a friend who does things that disappoint you. Have you boys ever had that happen to you?"

"Like when someone cheats at snakes and ladders?" asked Fred.

"Yes, Fred, it's like that."

"Papa, what did Stephen Douglas do to you?" asked Willie.

"He says things about me that he knows are untrue."

"That's not fair," replied Fred. "I wouldn't like a friend like that."

"Can you stop him from doing it?" asked Willie.

"Boys, the best thing is to beat him in an election, but I haven't done that yet."

Jesse scratched his head, wondering if I was giving the right message to the children. He wished me well in New York, and he and Fred went back to their morning chore.

I planned to leave Springfield for New York on February 22, George Washington's birthday.

Molly would not accompany me, as she was staying home with the boys.

Bob, who had failed the admissions tests for Harvard, was attending Phillips Academy in Exeter, New Hampshire, to prepare himself for a reapplication. Because I believed that no one at Harvard would have heard of Bob or me, in the midst of our political combat, I asked Judge Douglas to write a letter of recommendation for him. The Judge consented readily, and his secretary sent us a copy of his warm and convincing letter. Molly wrote to thank him, and I added a postscript that read, "I appreciate your personal kindness which transcends our present differences."

After the lecture in New York, my plan was to give follow-up speeches in two cities in Connecticut: Hartford and New Haven. I would then travel to Exeter to visit Bob. As it was his first extended period away from home, I looked forward to hearing his impressions of attending a boarding school in the East.

On the morning of February 22, there was no fanfare for me as I boarded the first train for State Line, Indiana. There I transferred to another line, the Toledo, Wabash & Western Railway for Ft. Wayne. I continued on the Pittsburgh, Fort Wayne and Chicago railway to Pittsburgh. Next came the transfer at Pittsburgh onto the train for Philadelphia. When I finally reached New York, late on the night of February 25, the trip had taken three days. I was exhausted, although I did have a day and a half to recover.

In 1857, when Molly and I visited New York, we stayed at the Astor House. Because I recalled it pleasantly, I decided I would stay there again. Late on the Saturday night when I arrived at the hotel, I climbed the stairs to my room, unlocked the door, and entered. It was a well-appointed suite with a high-poster mahogany bed, a large antique bureau, plush draperies, and elegant chairs that accommodated my long legs. I looked out the window and saw the moon shining brightly on the granite stones of my windowsill.

Before turning in for the night, I relaxed in one of the chairs and let my thoughts flow.

Though I had dealt with challenges all my life, I had now reached one where the outcome could determine my fate. If I wanted to be president, I would have to pass this test. The audience would be full of influential men who would be deciding whether I should be given serious consideration for the Republican nomination for president.

How would I be perceived in New York? I was competing with Senator Seward, Senator Chase, and Representative Bates for the highest prize in American politics. I was not as experienced or cultivated as any of them. If I could not overcome my image as a country bumpkin from the frontier, I would fail.

Surely when I debated Douglas, I was under the same intense scrutiny, but I was campaigning for the Senate and not the presidency. Seward and Douglas had sought the presidency all their lives. For me it was still fanciful, a dream that might well evaporate into the morning mist. I was not nervous as I came to this juncture in my life, but I was respectful of the talents, the qualities, and the abilities I would need to succeed.

This was a test I had to pass.

Chapter 16

I Believed My Country Needed Me

When I woke the next morning, I was surprised to learn from the newspapers I would not be speaking at Beecher's church, but that my lecture was now under the sponsorship of the Young Men's Central Republican Union, and that I would be speaking in the Great Hall at Cooper Union on 7th Street in Manhattan.

Because I postponed my lecture from November to late February, the elders of the Young Men's Union, Horace Greeley and William Cullen Bryant, who were both anti-Seward Republicans, were delighted to welcome me under their banner. Both were hopeful that by introducing me to a New York audience, the cause of Seward might be slowed, and those of Chase and Bates advanced. Greeley and Bryant were both editors of New York newspapers, and Bryant was an accomplished poet and the author of "Thanatopsis," the poem I had discovered and memorized in Robert Todd's library.

I was fortunate to have two days to revise the parts of my text that were more suited to a church congregation than a political audience. As both days before my evening lecture were filled with appointments and events, I had little time to stitch the changes into my speech.

The highlight of the second day was having my portrait taken by the noted photographer Mathew Brady. His latest portraits of Judge Douglas and Senator Seward hung in places of honor and were ready to adorn campaign banners. Brady said his most difficult problem with my portrait was how to make my new suit look less wrinkled.

I have to confess that as the hour approached for my speech, I grew more nervous. I simply had to trust my preparation, my composition, my rehearsals, and my delivery. The afternoon and early evening in New York were unusually mild, and a large crowd assembled in the hall.

After the dignitaries were seated on the speaker's platform, Bryant, the man who would introduce me, and I strode out toward the two seats next to the podium.

Bryant gave me a hearty welcome, and the podium was mine.

I looked out over the impassive faces and the steady glow of the gas lights, and began.

"MR. PRESIDENT AND FELLOW CITIZENS OF NEW YORK–"

It was hard not to be self-conscious. Compared to Bryant in his neat fitting suit, my new clothes hung on me like a scarecrow's. My voice was high-pitched, and I was sure they would find my Kentucky accent peculiar. At the beginning of any speech, my gestures were ill-timed. I just had to get started.

I began by giving the audience an introduction to my address.

"The facts with which I shall deal this evening are mainly old and familiar; nor is there anything new in the general use I shall make of them. If there shall be any novelty, it will be in the mode of presenting the facts, and the inferences and observations following that presentation."

To set the foundation upon which I would build my argument, I used a quote from Judge Douglas's recent speech in Columbus, Ohio.

"Our fathers, when they framed the Government under which we live, understood this question 'just as well, and even better, than we do now.'"

I continued by stating the question to which Douglas referred.

"What is the question those fathers understood, 'just as well, and even better than we do now?"

"It is this: Does the proper division of local from federal authority, or anything in the Constitution, forbid our federal government to control slavery in our federal territories?"

This, of course, was the question with which Douglas and I had wrestled in our debates. Was there anything in the Constitution that forbid the federal government to control slavery in the territories? Could police regulations framed by a local legislature forbid or allow slavery in the territories?

"Upon this, Senator Douglas holds the affirmative, and Republicans the negative. This affirmation and denial form an issue; and this issue–this question–is precisely what our fathers understood, 'better than we.'"

The audience cheered, and I now had my rhythm.

I then identified the men who signed the Constitution as the founders of our republic.

Among them were George Washington, James Madison, Alexander Hamilton, Benjamin Franklin, John Rutledge, and Charles Cotesworth Pinckney. I presented the evidence I had found of their voting records on issues relating to slavery when they served in the legislatures of the Articles of Confederation and under the Constitution.

After each of the citations of 21 of the founders' votes, I added:

"By this, he showed that in his understanding, no line dividing local from federal authority, nor anything in the Constitution, was violated by Congress."

Summarizing my research, I stated:

"The sum of the whole is, that of our 39 fathers who framed the original Constitution, 21–a clear majority of the whole–certainly understood that no proper division of local from federal authority, nor any part of the Constitution, forbade the Federal Government to control slavery in the federal territories . . . and Judge Douglas's text affirms that they understood the question 'better than we.'"

I'd trapped Douglas with his own argument!

The audience understood, and laughter and cheering rose and continued.

Concluding the first part of my address, I claimed:

"This is all Republicans ask–all Republicans desire–in relation to slavery. As those fathers marked it, so let it be again marked, as an evil not to be extended, but to be tolerated and protected only because of and so far as its actual presence among us makes that toleration and protection a necessity. Let all the guarantees those fathers gave it, be, not grudgingly, but fully and fairly, maintained. For this Republicans contend, and with this, so far as I know or believe, they will be content."

There was more applause.

I was now ready to begin the second part, which was about the dangers of sectional conflict and addressed to the southern people.

I declared we were not a sectional party. It was the South that rejected the national principle upon which the Republican Party was formed: that the federal government had the right to control slavery in the federal territories.

"If our principle, put in practice, would wrong your section for the benefit of ours, or for any other object, then our principle and we with it, are sectional, and are justly opposed and denounced as such. Meet us, then, on the question of whether our principle, put in practice, would wrong your section; do you accept the challenge? No! Then you really believe that the principle our fathers thought so clearly right is in fact so clearly wrong as to demand your condemnation."

I declared we were not a radical or revolutionary party, but a conservative party.

"But you say you are conservative–eminently conservative–while we are revolutionary, destructive, or something of the sort. What is conservatism? Is it not adherence to the old and tried against the new and untried? We stick to, contend for, the identical old policy on the point in the controversy which was adopted by 'our fathers who framed the Government under which we live;' while you with one accord reject and spit upon that old policy, and insist on substituting something new."

I replied to the charge that we were stirring up slave revolts and that John Brown was motivated by "Black Republican" ideas.

"You charge that we stir up insurrections among your slaves. We deny it; and what is your proof? Harpers Ferry! John Brown was no Republican; and you have failed to implicate a single Republican in his Harpers Ferry enterprise.

"John Brown's effort was peculiar. It was not a slave insurrection. It was an attempt by white men to get up a revolt among slaves, in which the slaves refused to participate. In fact, it was so absurd that the slaves, with all their ignorance, saw plainly enough it could not succeed."

I finished this section by responding to southern threats to destroy the Union if a Republican were elected president.

"Your purpose, then, plainly stated, is that you will destroy the Government, unless you be allowed to construe and enforce the Constitution as you please, on all points in dispute between you and us. You will rule or ruin in all events.

"But you will not abide the election of a Republican president! In that supposed event, you say, you will destroy the Union; and then, you say, the great crime of having destroyed it will be upon us!"

I closed with a few words addressed to my fellow Republicans.

"It is exceedingly desirable that all parts of this great Confederacy shall be at peace, and in harmony, one with another. Let us Republicans do our part to have it so.

"Our conviction is that slavery is wrong. If slavery is right, all words, acts, laws, and constitutions against it, are themselves wrong, and should be silenced and swept away. If it is right, we cannot justly object to its nationality; if it is wrong, they cannot justly insist upon its extension–its enlargement. All they ask, we could readily grant, if we thought slavery right; all we ask, they could as readily grant, if they thought it wrong. Their thinking it right, and our thinking it wrong, is the precise fact upon which depends the whole controversy.

"Thinking it wrong, as we do, can we yield to them? Can we cast our votes with their view, and against our own? In view of our moral, social, and political responsibilities, can we do this?"

There were cries of "No, no, never," and applause in the hall.

"Can we, while our votes will prevent it, allow it to spread into the National Territories, and to overrun us here in these Free States?"

Once again, there were cries of "No, no, never" in the hall.

"LET US HAVE FAITH THAT RIGHT MAKES MIGHT, AND IN THAT FAITH, LET US, TO THE END, DARE TO DO OUR DUTY AS WE UNDERSTAND IT."

When I finished, the crowd instantly rose to greet me with an ovation. People were applauding, cheering, yelling "huzzah" and "bravo," and waving handkerchiefs and hats.

It was continuous. The wave of energy, resounding through the hall and sweeping over the podium, vibrated through me. I waved back and held both my arms into the air. This caused even greater applause and spontaneous cheering. To have connected so effectively with this audience left me inspired and drained.

As the clamor gradually eased, Bryant stepped over to me, and said, "That was the best political speech I have ever heard in my life." The following morning the New York newspapers were equally generous in their praise.

I was now a serious candidate for the Republican nomination for president.

After my trip through New England, the highlight of which was seeing Bob and his friends at Exeter, I returned to Springfield. It was time for me to meet with my key advisors about the upcoming Republican Party events, the Illinois convention in Decatur, and the party's national convention in Chicago.

Davis had added Jesse Dubois, Stephen Logan, and Ward Hill Lamon to our core group. These men met with me in my office in early March. As I looked around the room, I thought about my relationship with each one. Our bonds were formed in our years in the state legislature, in our political activities afterward, but with many of them, in our time on the eighth circuit. In working together, traveling together, and laughing and living together, we had learned what was at the core of each man's character. We knew each other intimately. We trusted each other and believed in each other.

Sitting at the head of the green covered table, Davis breathed deeply, causing his chest and stomach to expand, looked out at us, and began, "We need to make several decisions this morning, but before we get to them, I will give you a brief report on the Democrats.

"Late next month, they will meet in Charleston to nominate their candidate for president. It looks as if they are careening toward chaos. Douglas still has his hold on the northern Democrats, but he is no longer trusted in the South. His support has dwindled, and a southern candidate will emerge. The newspapers are touting Breckenridge. If this happens, and most likely it will, there will be a deadlock. Barring one side compromising with the other, it will be insoluble."

"What will happen then?" asked Billy.

"They will probably split into two parties for this election," replied Judd firmly.

"Precisely," said Davis, "which means, gentlemen, that the Republican National Convention, that meets in Chicago in the middle of May, will be choosing the next president of the United States."

"Which will be Senator William H. Seward of New York," added Leonard Swett.

"Yes, Swett, always the realist," responded Davis.

"But he is right," added the newcomer Jesse Dubois. "Seward is the overwhelming favorite, and the newspapers are claiming he will win on the first ballot."

"Not all of them," said Billy. "Strangely enough, the papers that are against him are in New York!"

"Greeley!" shouted Davis. "He hates Seward and his inside man, Thurlow Weed. He's promoting Bates as a compromise candidate."

Dubois spoke up again, "Lincoln should be the compromise candidate."

"Which brings me to the main point of this morning's meeting," bellowed Davis. "Here it is, March 7, with our national nominating convention set to open on Wednesday, May 16, and we don't even know if we have a candidate."

The room was silent.

"Lincoln," said Davis, "you can no longer hesitate. You have come to your 'To be or not to be' moment. Do you want us to proceed on your behalf to secure the Republican presidential nomination?"

Here it was. The time to choose.

Since I'd not served as an executive in political office, I'd not had to make decisions like this.

I did know one thing. After the debacle of breaking my engagement to Molly, I'd sworn to stand firm by a decision once I'd gone through an extensive process of making it.

I'd shied away from making a decision under the cover of not being a contender. Cooper Union stripped that from me.

In the months leading up to Cooper Union, I'd found the taste to be in my mouth, but this called for more than just a taste.

Anyone making a decision like this, aware that it might come to fruition, could not proceed without an awareness of his flaws, but he must be equally aware of his strengths.

It meant offering all of myself as the person I had become.

Could I do that?

I did my best not to make a decision based on arrogance, pride, or ambition.

I believed my country needed me.

It was from this certainty that my confidence arose.

I did not know what my country and I would face, but with God's guidance and protection we could not fail.

I looked at each of them, and with a mixture of fear, humility, and confidence, I calmly said, "I do."

There was what I could only describe as a common exhale. Then came the nods, the congratulations, the banter, and the laughter.

"Thank goodness that's out of the way," said Davis. "Now we have to focus on Decatur and making sure Lincoln is chosen as the favorite son candidate of Illinois." With that the judge adjourned the meeting.

I arrived late for the evening session on the first day of the Decatur convention. As the speeches droned on, Dick Oglesby, a younger Republican friend of mine from Decatur, ascended the rostrum to give the next speech.

As he began, he announced, "I am informed that a distinguished citizen of Illinois, and one of whom Illinois ever delights to honor, is present, and I wish to move that this body invite him to a seat on the stand."

To build the suspense, Dick did not immediately name "this distinguished citizen."

Finally, he shouted, "Abraham Lincoln!"

At this point, the cheering crowd spotted me, and as the convention hall erupted, they carried me up to the main platform.

Oglesby continued, "There is an old Democrat of Macon County who desired to make a contribution to the Convention."

The crowd yelled, "Receive it!"

I had no idea what was happening.

From the back of the hall, my cousin John Hanks from Decatur, who was by now an old man, and a friend came forward with two fence rails.

A large cardboard sign identified them as:

Abraham Lincoln, The Rail Candidate for President in 1860

Two rails from a Lot of 3,000 Made in 1830 by Thos. Hanks and Abe Lincoln—

Whose Father was the First Pioneer of Macon County.

The convention exploded with demonstrations of support for the Rail Candidate. In the tumult, a small part of the roof fell down on the crowd. When it was removed, I was called on to speak.

I was nonplussed, but I managed a few words.

"I suppose I am expected to reply to that. I cannot say whether I made those rails, but I can say that I've mauled many and better ones since I've grown to manhood."

I did not point out that the sign painter had mistaken Thos. for John Hanks and that my father was not the first pioneer in the county.

The crowd loved it all the more, and henceforth I was known as "the Rail-splitter."

The convention got down to business the following day.

Thanks to the efforts of John Palmer, they adopted this resolution.

" . . . that Abraham Lincoln is the first choice of Illinois for the presidency, and that our delegates be instructed to use all honorable means for his nomination by the Chicago convention, and to cast their votes as a unit for him."

Chapter 17

I'll Go Down and Tell Her

After the Decatur convention, Davis and I returned to his house in Bloomington, where I stayed over with Sarah and him.

The next morning Sarah served us a hearty breakfast. I ate sparingly, but Davis devoured his oatmeal, eggs, toast, and sausage. We thanked Sarah, and he and I carried our cups of coffee into his study.

He turned his comfortable desk chair around to face me as I sat on the leather sofa.

Davis leaned back, patted his stomach, and said, "A bit different from our days on the circuit, don't you think?"

"Indeed it is," I replied.

Turning to what lay ahead, he observed, "We've made it over the first hurdle, albeit a small one."

"It was important, and if I had failed, it would have been over."

"Right, so on to what comes next. Today is Friday. Tomorrow we head to Chicago for the national convention. We'll get settled in the Tremont Hotel, review the instructions, and begin the hunt for delegates. They start arriving on Sunday, and the campaign teams will be all over them. The meetings with operatives, the caucuses, the buttonholing, and the arm twisting will last until the balloting on Thursday night or Friday morning."

"Do you have any feel for where we are?"

"Do you want the truth?"

"Of course."

"Seward is the overwhelming favorite. Our chances of overtaking him are minimal. Nonetheless, we have a strategy, and we have a good team. Hubris has led to the downfall of many good men. It looks, however, that under Thurlow Weed, they are a disciplined team close to the victory they've been tasting for years."

"And what is our strategy?"

"First we have to dislodge some of Seward's delegates. We'll work with our friends in the key states. We may have to join together with the Bates and Chase men to slow down Seward. Our goal will be to stop him from winning on the first ballot."

"Is there a chance of that?"

"I think there is. Seward is the leader of the party, and many of the delegates will believe he deserves the nomination. He has the momentum, but he has flaws. He is perceived as radical on slavery. There are doubts that Seward can carry the swing states—New Jersey, Pennsylvania, Indiana, and Illinois. Although Weed is the emblem of propriety, there is a hint of corruption in Seward's realm. There are chinks in the armor, and we have to expose them. The Bates and Chase men are with us on doing that."

"If we keep him from winning on the first ballot, what happens next?"

"There are 465 delegates; a majority is 233. In addition to slowing down Seward, we need to win 100 delegates for you on the first ballot."

"How many do we have now."

"As of this moment, we have 22, the delegates from the state of Illinois, and we have them for one ballot."

"How do we get the other 80?"

"We dig in for four days of hard work. We do it delegation by delegation. Indiana is the linchpin. We have to show we can win delegates in states other than our own. There are twenty-five on our team. I will send them out in groups of two or three to meet with the delegations, and then individual delegates. You have made a number of good friends over the years, and we will depend on them. Some of them are in unlikely places, Tuck, for instance in New Hampshire."

"Yes, he served with me in Congress."

"Seward will not know that we are gradually undermining him. The Indiana delegation is where we begin."

"Col. Lane is their candidate for governor, and he hates Seward."

"Yes, there's plenty of that. Your boyhood and teenage connection to Indiana also helps. We'll have to work with Caleb Smith, which is not easy. We have friends of yours working for us in other New England states, and in Virginia, Kentucky, and Pennsylvania. We will not sleep much, but the goal is to harvest 100 delegates for you on the first ballot."

"If we get that far it will be a miracle."

"No, that's just the first step. Over the four days, our primary goal will be to make you everyone's second choice. If Seward can be stopped, we believe the convention will turn to you."

"Not Chase?"

"No, too radical. and doesn't connect with people. He's had a bad case of presidential fever for years, so he will be surprised to learn his enthusiasm is not shared by many others."

"Not Bates?"

"I don't think so, but that's a tougher one. Greeley and Frank Blair are pushing him. He does have some appeal as a compromise candidate. He comes from Missouri, which is an advantage if the delegates want a western man. He's probably too conservative on slavery, and he suffers from his association with the Know Nothings. The Germans and other immigrants will never vote for him."

"And Lincoln?"

"You are positioned perfectly. You were born in the South, lived in Indiana, and, of course, Illinois. Your views on slavery, which you formed over the years, and defined so clearly at Cooper Union, are free from the taint of abolition; you are right on the tariff, the homestead, and internal improvements; you are "Honest Old Abe," a man of the people, and electable. That's what they want—someone who can win and who can strengthen the ticket in each of their states."

"So what happens if we get this far?"

"It will be all about momentum. We want you to peak on Thursday, not before. We don't want the others to unite around stopping you. Judd deserves credit for the brilliant move of bringing the convention to Chicago. He has a floor map that will isolate the Seward delegations. They'll be trapped and unable to communicate with their leaders in the other states when they realize what is happening.

"We have a plan to pack the galleries for you when the balloting begins. In a place like the Wigwam, the noise will be deafening."

"You are to make no commitments for me which I would be loath to keep. I know there will be horse trading, but I do not want my hands tied," I said sternly.

"We will do our best."

"And what about me?"

"You have the most difficult part of it all."

"What is that?"

"You do nothing! You must know the tradition that no candidate is to be present at the nominating convention."

"I do know that. Douglas violated it last month."

"It didn't do him any good. They were hurtling toward a split, and now he is the official leader of half the Democracy. I should have congratulated you. You have vanquished the Little Giant."

"I bear no credit for that, and I wouldn't want it. Douglas vanquished himself."

"Nonetheless, you will stay in Springfield and do nothing. Play games of fives, have fun with your boys, sit by the fireplace with your wife, take walks, and read the newspapers—even though they will be a day late with the news."

"How will I know what is happening?"

"You won't. We will do our job. Trust us. We will write letters which you will receive the next day, we will send telegrams which you will receive in thirty minutes, and we may send someone down on the night train for Thursday. The events will break quickly, so you may not know one way or the other on Thursday night or Friday morning."

"I am forever grateful to all of you, and to you, in particular."

"You have our thanks, and our commitment to making you the next president of the United States. But remember Lincoln, our chances are minimal."

"Godspeed, Davis."

He was right. As Saturday arrived and gave way to Sunday, the waiting was unbearable. And it was just beginning.

Molly and I sat by the fireplace after supper on Sunday and tried to relax. We had heard nothing.

"You must try to take your mind off it," she advised me.

"Molly, you of all people know that is impossible."

"When do you think we shall hear from them?"

"I'd be surprised if we didn't get a letter from Davis tomorrow. His letters are terse, so I am not sure we will learn much. Delahay is more chatty, but he sways with the moment. The same is true for Dubois, but he's more reliable. Judd knows what's happening, but he never writes. We'll just have to piece it together."

"I have no doubt that you will be nominated and elected."

"And why is that?"

"Because ever since I was a girl, I knew I would marry a president."

"And I always said you'd missed your chance when you passed on Douglas."

"That was a long time ago, and you are close to it, while he is left with nothing."

"Remember, Molly, Seward has the backing, he has the momentum, and Davis warned us our chances were minimal."

"Trust me, Mr. Lincoln, they will turn to you."

Molly's confidence was heartening, but I could not shake my sense that this could be another failure. I had thrown myself into the two Senate races, and both times I had been agonizingly close to winning. This was for an even greater prize. The road was littered with the carcasses of men who had been bitten by the presidential bug and lost. How could I succeed when so many of them had failed?

The forces at the highest level of the political world would align themselves against me.

At my deepest, I still regarded winning the nomination as unimaginable, but perhaps this thought was protection against the fear of another failure. I did not think I could give my fullest to another political contest and lose again. In 1855 and 1858, it took months to pull free from the depression that threatened to overwhelm me. What would it be like this time?

And then it came to me.

"There is providence in the fall of a sparrow."

Where was that from?

Hamlet!

It was Hamlet before he made his decision.

And then came the words, "The readiness is all."

And the final question:

Are you ready?

And my answer was, "Yes, I am."

And so I remained calm in the knowledge that if this were to come, it would be providential, and I would be ready.

On Monday morning we had our first letter from Judge Davis.

Sunday, May 13

Lincoln,

DAMN!

Someone forgot to reserve rooms for us at the Tremont. We were almost out on the street until I found my friend, Drake, the assistant manager. He procured us rooms, but we had to pay extra for "the evacuation of certain rooms by private families."

I have taken charge, and am in suite 74, with a sign on my door, "Illinois Headquarters."

Davis

I frowned at Molly.

"If this is what we hear from Davis all week, I will not be pleased. How can he expect us to be patient when this is all we hear?"

"Wait until the others write or telegram. Perhaps events are flowing too swiftly for even them to follow."

Molly was right.

On Tuesday morning we did hear from the others.

In the morning mail were letters from my longtime friend Nathan Knapp and Amos Tuck.

May 14

Dear Sir:

Things are working; keep a good nerve—be not surprised at any result—but I want to tell you that your chances are not the worst. We have got Seward in the attitude of the representative Republican of the East—you of the West. We are laboring to make you the second choice of all the Delegations we can where we cannot make you first choice. We are dealing tenderly with delegates, taking them in detail, and making no fuss. Be not too Expectant but rely upon our discretion. Again I say brace your nerves for any result. truly your friend

N.M. Knapp

May 14

My Dear Sir:

I take great satisfaction in assuring you, that what I hoped might be practicable, when I left home, seems to me when here, to be within the range of decided possibilities—I mean your nomination as Pres—I believe it desirable for our party, and our principles, for you to be put on the track—I am taking hold of hands with our N. Eng. delegates, and find the prospect good for general co-operation—Be not misled by our first votes—it will be expedient not to strike at first, but to let the west make the first move—But we shall come "on time-"

Your son was at my house, at tea, the evening before I left home (last Wednesday)—he was in good health and spirits, and I hope he will feel at home at my door, while he remains in Exeter—He is a promising Son—Shall be happy to hear from you—with much regard

I am Yrs. Sincerely,

Amos Tuck—

On Tuesday afternoon, I decided to take Davis's advice and return to the fives court. It was much more glamorous than when we started playing the game there almost twenty years earlier.

Then I had competed almost daily with Billy Herndon, Joshua Speed, Ned Baker, John Hardin, and Jim Matheny. Most of them had left Springfield, and one of them was dead. It was a young man's game, and we were all good at it.

I had not played in several years because I had been so busy with politics and law cases, but on this day, I was ready to give it another try. It turned out I was not as rusty as I thought.

I joined the young group of Springfield professionals for several games. The fiercest competitors were the lawyers.

I served with the same power I'd always had, walloping returns at the wall, placing softer shots carefully to keep them from being returned, and loping and racing all over the court without smashing into the others. In my best playing days, my friends complained that I pushed the rules against physical contact.

After playing several games I had worn myself out, and walked slowly back home.

Molly greeted me and said the postman had brought a letter from Delahay. We sat down by the fireplace, and I opened it and read it to her.

May 14

Dear Lincoln

Things are working admirably well now. The Stock is gradually "rising." Indiana is all right, Ohio is prepared to do a good part after Chase has had his compliments paid him, New Hampshire and a part of N Jersey are talking out for you—also Mass—"Cottonwood" made a splendid hit in a German meeting today—they all conceed that you can easily be nominated for Vice President, but we are not biting at the Bait—in case you are nominated you must come up upon a request and address the Delegates at the "Wig Wam; you need have no fears about offending anyone. In Haste with high hopes.

Truly yours Delahay

When I finished Delahay's letter, I rose from my chair and stood in front of the fireplace.

Molly stayed seated and looked up at me.

"I have to go up there. I can take the early train tomorrow morning."

"Husband, this is so hard for you, but this letter is from Delahay. You've said he's inexperienced and excitable. He's devoted to you as are the others, but where is your good sense? You cannot go up there unless you hear from Davis."

It was difficult for me to say, but I had to agree with her.

"Yes, Molly, you are right. Your judgment is better than mine."

On Wednesday morning we had another letter from Davis. It was as if he had read my mind.

May 15

Lincoln

We have the Indiana delegation. Seward is throwing money and favors at undecided delegations. Don't come here unless we send for you. Can't send anyone down. All hands on deck.

Davis

Late that afternoon we had a telegram from Davis and Jesse Dubois.

May 16

To A Lincoln

The are quiet but moving heaven & Earth nothing will beat us but old fogy politicians the heart of the delegates are with us.

Davis & Dubois

I went for a walk, and when I returned it was time for supper with Molly and the boys.

When I entered the kitchen, I asked Molly if there was any news from Chicago, and she replied there was none.

We sat down at the family table and dove into our salads with lettuce from the garden in back of the house.

When we had finished, Willie looked over at me and said, "Papa, Mama says you will be president of the United States."

"William Wallace," I said, "your mother has been convinced that she would be married to a president since she was a little girl."

"Will we have to leave Springfield if you are the . . . what's it called? What is it, Willie?" asked Tad.

Molly laughed at them and said, "Boys, there is a very important meeting that is going on in Chicago, and it may change our lives."

"And it may not," I added.

"What does the president do, Papa?" inquired Willie.

"Well, son, I don't rightly know, but we may find out if your mother is right."

"Where does the 'presdinet' live?" asked Tad.

"Taddy, he lives in Washington in a house that is all white."

"Is it big?"

"Oh, yes," I replied, "and you would have lots of rooms to play in and important people to chase after. One of them is even called Senator Chase, although I don't think he likes children. And you could run around in the big yard with ponies and wagons and goats."

"Father!" cautioned Molly.

"When will we know?" asked Willie excitedly.

"Soon," said Molly, "and you'll have to wait just like us."

Thursday was the day when the anticipation became even greater. If all went well for the Seward forces, the balloting could begin that night, and the nomination would, in all likelihood, be his. Every delay gave my friends more opportunity to pry delegates loose from Seward. We were hoping the balloting would be on Friday morning.

Molly and I took a walk to the Sangamon River and visited the spot where we had first become engaged. We brought a picnic lunch. It was a lovely spring day with colorful flowers and fresh green leaves swaying in a light breeze. We had commemorated so many events by the river, from Eddy's passing to the births of Willie and Tad. We mourned the loss of her father and of our friend John Hardin in the Mexican War. It was a place where the events of lifc took on perspective as we watched the water flow past.

In the afternoon we returned home, and I read the day's newspapers by the fireplace. There was nothing to give me a sense one way or the other.

In the early evening came both a letter and a telegram from Davis.

I read Molly the letter first.

May 16

Lincoln

A horse race. Seward in the lead. Don't want to draw even too early. Bide your time. Meet Thursday night with three top men from Indiana, New Jersey, Pennsylvania, and Illinois delegations. Not yet at 100 delegates on the first ballot.

Davis

Then the telegram.

May 17

To A Lincoln

Am very hopeful don't get Excited nearly dead with fatigue telegraph or write here very little.

Davis

We slept very little on Thursday night. We hadn't heard directly, but we believed the balloting would take place the following morning.

After breakfast on Friday, I walked to the telegraph office where I would wait for the results. When I arrived, the room was already full of friends. They greeted me warmly, and then let me sit quietly at first to read the morning *Illinois State Journal*.

On the second page was a dispatch that a reporter had written in Chicago on Thursday night—less than ten hours earlier.

Chicago, May 17, 1860, 10 p.m.

Special to the *Illinois State Journal*

The city is in an uproar tonight, and an "irrepressible conflict" appears to be raging between the friends of Lincoln and Seward. Their names are the only ones now mentioned in connection with the nomination for President, all others having been thrown off the track.

The balloting will commence in the morning as soon as the convention meets. Of course there will be a great deal of work done tonight, and the skillful and practical New Yorkers are active and confident of success. Their organization is well-drilled, powerful, and united, and its influence is felt in every direction.

A tremendous outside pressure is at work in Seward's favor which would dampen the ardor of men less earnest and bold than the friends of Lincoln. His interests are confided to hands that lack neither judgment nor pluck, and he will not be abandoned while there is a ray of hope. Whatever the result, they deserve the cordial thanks of every friend of the noble Lincoln for the adroitness displayed in guarding his interests.

At 10:30, the results of the first ballot came over the machine. The operator read us the numbers:

William H. Seward, New York	173 1/2
Abraham Lincoln, Illinois	102
Edward Bates, Missouri	48
Simon Cameron, Pennsylvania	50 1/2
John McLean, Ohio	12
Salmon P. Chase, Ohio	49
Benjamin F. Wade, Ohio	3
William L. Dayton, New Jersey	14
John M. Reed, Pennsylvania	1
Jacob Collamer, Vermont	10
Charles Sumner, Massachusetts	1
John C. Fremont	1

I was standing next to my friend Charles Zane and said to him, "I don't like the looks of it; I imagine that about forty of those votes were cast for me by men who supposed they were bound to give me an empty compliment on the first ballot. They were cast, according to my figuring, by friends of Wade and Bates. If so, if I lose them on the next ballot, the nomination will also be lost."

At noon came the results of the second ballot.

William H. Seward, New York	184 1/2
Abraham Lincoln, Illinois	181
Edward Bates, Missouri	35
Simon Cameron, Pennsylvania	2
John McLean, Ohio	8
Salmon P. Chase	42 1/2
William L. Dayton, New Jersey	10
Cassius M. Clay, Kentucky	2

Zane looked at me for my reaction and I told him, "I think the convention will nominate me on the next ballot."

The numbers from the third ballot would arrive in an hour. I walked next door to the office of the *Illinois State Journal* where more of my friends were chatting with each other. They greeted me heartily, and I enjoyed the company as I waited for the results.

An hour later, a messenger boy from the telegraph office brought me a telegram.

May 18 1860
Caton Lines
Illinois and Mississippi Telegraph Company
By telegraph from Chicago to Abraham Lincoln
Your nominated
J.J. Richards

When the boy gave it to me, everyone could tell from my face what it said, but they waited for me to read it, and I did, "You're nominated."

I might have turned a bit pale, but I know I trembled. As my friends congratulated me, I tried to thank them as graciously as I could, but then I said, "There's a little woman down at our house who would like to hear this. I'll go down and tell her."

Chapter 18

The Sweep of Events

It was hard to believe the Republican Party had nominated me for president. A mere eighteen months earlier I had lost the Senate election to Stephen Douglas. My political career was finished. This reversal in my fortune was difficult to comprehend.

Since I thought I'd had little or no chance to win the nomination, and since the idea of becoming president had budded so recently, I was not yet accustomed to it. The sweep of events continuing to propel me forward was so forceful and consuming that it kept other thoughts at bay.

I was in awe at being chosen to contend for the highest office in the country. David Davis and my friends flawlessly executed their strategy for winning the nomination. I owed so much to them. After our years together on the eighth circuit and in Illinois politics they believed in my capability to lead our country. That alone was humbling.

On June 18, the Democrats reconvened their convention in Baltimore. They could not resolve their differences, and the southern Democrats walked out and held their own convention at a nearby location. This formal split resulted in Douglas's nomination by the northerners and John C. Breckenridge's by the southerners.

At the same time, conservative Whigs and Know Nothings, who would not vote for me, or either Douglas or Breckenridge, formed a Constitutional Union Party with the goal of preventing disunion. Their candidate was John Bell, who had been a Whig senator from Tennessee and an opponent of the Kansas-Nebraska Act. Bell's support would probably come from the border states.

As June came to a close, there were four tickets in the race for president.

The tradition in presidential campaigns was for the candidates to remain at home while the leading politicians of each party travelled the country making speeches on the candidates' behalf. Fortunately, my former rivals from the convention in Chicago, William Henry Seward, Salmon Chase, and Edward Bates, accepted this responsibility gladly. We were now united in our quest for a Republican victory in November.

Newspaper articles and editorials also did their best to tilt the voters one way or the other. In Springfield, the *Illinois State Journal* endorsed me, while the *Illinois State Register* came out for Douglas.

It was hard for me to sit tight in Springfield.

As time wore on, I was haunted by thoughts of losing once again. I would be locked in another bitter contest with Stephen Douglas. How could I be sure he wouldn't win by an eyelash as he had before?

I could not banish the doubts from my mind. If I did not win, I would fail in my last effort to attain political success, and I would let down my party, and all those delegates who believed in me.

When I felt this way, I went for a long walk along the paths through the prairie near Springfield. Although it was hot, the green grasses swayed softly in the morning breeze. With the sun arching higher in the bright, blue sky, I felt the strength and permanence of the prairie. It had been like this for hundreds of years, and it would be this way for hundreds more. I opened myself to this lesson from the land.

After living with melancholy all my life, I had learned to take one step forward, followed by the next one, and to continue the journey. I did not know if I would be president, or what would come in the years ahead, but it was invigorating to have a role in national events.

Because I was confined to Springfield, Molly became my confidante. Each evening after the boys were asleep, we sat in our comfortable chairs by the fireplace and talked into the late evening.

"I think Willie is the one who is most like you," she said.

"What makes you think that?" I replied.

Her eyes sparkled as she sat forward in her chair.

She started, "He takes in everything and thinks carefully about it, just like you. He's kind and genial to the neighbors, and he loves to make people laugh. You should have seen him yesterday with Jesse Dubois. It was like two grown ups who'd known each other for years."

"What were they talking about?" I asked.

"Why, what it will be like when you're president, of course! Willie was asking Jesse who he would put in the cabinet."

"Maybe both of them know more about it than I do."

"Perhaps not. Willie wanted Billy the Barber to be the secretary of the treasury."

"That's not so far fetched. Billy is very good with money. He already owns a block of Springfield. What did Jesse say to that?"

"He went into the notion that you might have to choose some people to whom you are already beholden, and Billy wasn't one of them."

"Billy would be a sight better than Simon Cameron or Caleb Smith, but, my dear, we're getting ahead of ourselves."

"This is so hard for you, but you will win, and we will be living in the White House."

"The outlook for the Republicans is favorable," I replied, "but we've both known times when it comes undone, sometimes at the very end."

"What are you worried about?" she asked.

"The feuds between the Republican factions in Pennsylvania and New York—and word is getting back to us about wrangling in Indiana as well. We need those three states to be elected outright."

"Right," Molly replied, "if none of you wins a majority in the electoral college, it goes to the House of Representatives. If Douglas wins New York and if Bell wins the border states, there won't be a path to a majority for you. Douglas will have a good chance if it goes to the House."

She gave me a look of concern.

"Yes," I said, "there is more. The radical elements in the South are threatening that if a Republican is elected president, they will secede from the Union. They continue to tar us as a radical abolitionist party. That could scare off some voters. We'll just have to see."

"What have you done to prevent that?"

"I've referred them all back to my record, to my speeches and statements of the past six years. I have made it clear I will do nothing to slavery in the South, and I will enforce the Fugitive Slave Act. They don't trust me, and they know I am unalterably opposed to letting it extend into the territories. They simply believe that one day I will be coming for them. There is nothing I can do to allay their fears."

"So it's not certain we will win?"

"Absolutely not."

"Is there anything more you can do?"

"My task is to hold the Republican Party together."

I devoted myself to lengthy correspondence with Republican leaders in each state. I tried to learn what issues were most important to the residents in their states, and if a letter from me could give them reassurance. To help me with my correspondence, I was able to hire John Nicolay, whom I'd known in his role as custodian of Illinois state election records.

John Wood, the governor of Illinois, encouraged me to use the governor's room in the State Capitol building as my office. It became the headquarters of my campaign for president. I could meet with politicians from across the country and address groups of visitors gathered on the second-floor landing and the staircase.

During the summer the feud in Pennsylvania continued to simmer.

In the Chicago convention, Pennsylvania's delegation had turned the momentum toward my nomination. We needed the same wave to break for me in the general election. The factions were at each other's throats. One of them was led by Senator Simon Cameron and the other by the Republican candidate for governor, Andrew Curtin.

There were several issues, but the most spiteful was the charge that Cameron was hopelessly corrupt. This had been whispered for years, but the Curtin faction wanted to take it a step further. I wrote to John M. Pomeroy, "My sincere wish is that both sides will allow by-gones to be by-gones, and look to the present and future only."

In New York, tension brewed between Seward and the influential newspapermen Horace Greeley and William Cullen Bryant. This threatened to erupt just as Douglas realized the election could be decided by New York's electoral votes. I wrote to Thurlow Weed on August 17, warning him, "I think there will be the most extraordinary effort ever made, to carry New York for Douglas. You, and all the others who write me from your state, think the effort cannot succeed; and I hope you are right. Still it will require close watching."

Toward the end of the summer, we learned that Douglas was breaking the tradition that presidential candidates refrain from campaigning. He launched an extensive speaking tour through states in both the North and the South. He felt it could tip the scale in his favor if the election were close. I agreed, and it made me even more restless to be restricted to Springfield.

On August 17, I wrote to James F. Simmons, a U.S. senator from Rhode Island.

Hon. J. F. Simmons

My dear Sir

I had not heard a word from Rhode-Island for a long time, till this morning, when I received a letter intimating that Douglas is enlisting some rich men there, who know how to use money, and that it is endangering the State. How is this? Please write me.

Yours truly

A. Lincoln

Our hopes were boosted by Republican victories in the local elections in Vermont and Maine in August. It was the first definite sign that we were well-positioned for success in the November general election, although we were still concerned about achieving a majority in the electoral college.

October brought good news as well. Republicans won most of the elections in the state contests in Pennsylvania, Ohio, and Indiana. We were cheered by those results, particularly from Pennsylvania, since those were states we had to win if I were to be elected president.

Simmering through the last weeks of the campaign were threats of what would happen in the South if I were elected—everything from resistance to the government to outright secession. A number of friends and Republican political leaders wrote encouraging me to reassure the southerners about our conservative position on slavery.

I wrote to George T. M. Davis with my response.

Private and Confidential

Geo. T. M. Davis, Esq

October 27. 1860

My dear Sir:

Mr. Dubois has shown me your letter of the 20th.; and I promised to write you. What is it I could say which would quiet alarm? Is it that no interference by the government, with slaves or slavery within the states, is intended? I have said this so often already, that a repetition of it is but mockery, bearing an appearance of weakness and cowardice, which perhaps should be avoided. Why do not uneasy men read what I have already said? and what our platform says? If they will not read or heed, then would they read, or heed, a repetition of them? Of course the declaration that there is no intention to interfere with slaves or slavery, in the states, with all that is fairly implied in such declaration, is true; and I should have no objection to make and repeat the declaration a thousand times, if there were no danger of encouraging bold bad men to believe they are dealing with one who can be scared into anything.

Yours very truly

A. Lincoln

In October, I also received a letter from Grace Bedell from Westfield, Chatauque County, in New York.

Hon A B Lincoln

Dear Sir

My father has just home from the fair and brought home your picture and Mr. Hamlin's. I am a little girl only eleven years old, but want you should be President of the United States very much so I hope you wont think me very bold to write to such a great man as you are. Have you any little girls about as large as I am if so give them my love and tell her to write to me if you cannot answer this letter. I have got 4 brother's and part of them will vote for you any way and if you will let your whiskers grow I will try and get the rest of them to vote for you   you would look a great deal better for your face is so thin. All the ladies like whiskers and they would tease their husband's to vote for you and then you would be President. My father is going to vote for you and if I was a man I would vote for you to but I will try and get every one to vote for you that I can I think that rail fence around your picture make it look very pretty   I have got a little baby sister she is nine weeks old and is just as cunning as can be. When you direct your letter direct to Grace Bedell Westfield Chatauque County New York

I must not write any more   answer this letter right off

Good bye

Grace Bedell

I wrote to Grace in return.

To Grace Bedell

Private

Miss. Grace Bedell

Springfield, Ills.

My dear little Miss.

Your very agreeable letter of the 15th. is received.

I regret the necessity of saying I have no daughters. I have three sons—one 17, one 9, and one 7, years of age. They, with their mother, constitute my whole family.

As to the whiskers, having never worn any, do you not think people would call it a piece of silly affection if I were to begin it now? Your very sincere well-wisher

A. Lincoln

Our hopes were high as Election Day neared. On Tuesday, November 6, it arrived.

In the morning, I walked to the Lincoln and Herndon law office. As ever, Billy awaited me with the newspapers and a cup of coffee. He was confident we would win, but I ventured no prediction. Too often I had been sure of an outcome that did not happen. We would have to wait by the telegraph for the votes to come in.

We had a steady flow of visitors all morning. At noon Billy and I adjourned for lunch. I ordered a hard-boiled egg and an apple, and he indulged his hearty appetite with beef stew.

As we finished with coffee, Billy looked over at me and said, "Lincoln, is it true that you will not vote for yourself today?"

"Yes, William, it is true. You know the tradition that nominees for president don't campaign and don't vote."

"I do, but aren't you the person who should end that silly practice?"

"No, I don't feel comfortable doing that."

"So you won't vote at all? What about all the other Republicans who are running for office in Illinois. Some of them are in close races."

"How can I do that?"

He took out a long narrow piece of paper, and said, "Let me show you."

He ripped off the top of the ballot where the voter was to choose the electors pledged to vote for the presidential and vice-presidential candidates.

"That's all there is to it," he grinned at me.

In the afternoon, Billy and I walked to the courthouse and cast our ballots. In front of the crowd who had gathered to wish me well, I detached the top of my sheet and placed the ballot in the box.

I had time for a game of fives, and then returned home for an early supper. After that it was over to the State Capitol building at 7 o'clock to await the early results.

Davis had prepared tally sheets for each state on which we could keep track of the votes. We were in the governor's room in the early evening, and relied on runners from the telegraph office.

The first returns came from Illinois. Most of them showed slightly increased Republican totals from those of the most recent election. We opened up healthy leads in Maine, Connecticut, Massachusetts, Rhode Island, New Hampshire, Vermont, and Pennsylvania. As the first votes from the Midwestern states rolled in, we led in Iowa, Michigan, Minnesota, and Wisconsin. Ohio and Indiana were closer than expected. Breckenridge was sweeping the South, and showing surprising strength in Ohio, Wisconsin, and Pennsylvania. He and Bell were contesting the border states. I received no votes in the South except a smattering of support in Kentucky, the place of my birth.

When we took a short break, Davis said, "It looks good in places, Lincoln, but it's very early."

At 9 o'clock, we walked over to the telegraph office. Davis was clutching his tally sheets in both hands. We expected most of the vote to be in by midnight.

A large crowd had gathered inside and outside the telegraph office. Three clerks were deciphering the flood of incoming votes. The crowd parted for Davis and me to sit next to the machines and the clerks. With every announcement of the vote totals, the crowd cheered or groaned.

As the evening wore on, we had a clearer view of the unfolding results.

I had strong leads in New England and many of the northern states, Breckenridge had won the South, and he and Bell were still contesting the border states. Douglas was running strongly in New York, he had surged ahead of me in Illinois, and he had a slight lead in Missouri.

Davis and I remained hopeful, but it was still possible I would not win a majority.

"It depends where these votes are coming from," said Davis. "The early votes were from the cities, and the rural vote is now trickling in. I am surprised Douglas is ahead of you in Illinois; that's not good. You are losing New Jersey, but Indiana is still in play. If we hold Illinois and Indiana, it will all come down to New York. It's much closer than we expected."

It was closing in on midnight, and I could do nothing but wait with my friends in the telegraph office. While I was used to waiting for the vote in close elections, I could not conceal how anxious I was about this one.

At 1 o'clock, before Davis and I could hear the clerk's voice, a huge cheer erupted from the crowd in the office, and it grew even louder as it rolled out into the crowd on the street. We had won Indiana and squeaked past Douglas in Illinois.

It all came down to New York.

Over the noise of the animated crowd, an exuberant Davis yelled, "If we win New York, we have a majority. You have 145 electoral votes; the others have 123. Majority is 152. New York has 35 votes. If you win it, we are at 180, if you lose, their total is 158."

I was almost numb. If I could not control my feelings, I could try to ignore them.

All evening we had held a small lead in New York, although it was not large enough to withstand a final surge for Douglas. We expected the last votes to be reported by 2 o'clock.

To break the tension, I decided to go outside and talk to my friends and neighbors. Everyone was awake with me awaiting the result. Although they were as nervous as I, we chatted amiably.

The conversations took my mind off the clicking telegraph, the first reactions of the clerks, and the expressions on Davis's face. I almost forgot the election returns.

Not for long. Suddenly the crowd inside the office exploded with a tumultuous roar.

We all knew what had happened. We had carried New York.

In what was left of the night, Springfield burst into ecstatic celebrations. Bands played, cannons boomed, spontaneous demonstrations erupted in the streets, and I was carried by the crowd around the town square.

Finally I was able to climb down and shout to them, "I have to tell my wife."

One of the men surrounding me called, "I think she knows by now."

Indeed she did, but when I arrived home, that did not stop me from embracing her and exclaiming, "Molly, Molly, we are elected!"

Chapter 19

Let It Hang There Undisturbed

Hon. Abraham Lincoln
President-elect of the United States
November 6, 1861

Sir:

Congratulations on your election. I stand ready to support you however I can.

S. A. Douglas

In the months that preceded my inauguration, the unthinkable happened. Between December 20, 1860, and February 1, 1861, South Carolina, Mississippi, Florida, Alabama, Georgia, Louisiana, and Texas seceded from the Union.

During this time a number of compromise plans emerged to keep more states from seceding, and to encourage the others to return. Some included constitutional amendments allowing slavery expansion.

I held to the position I outlined in letters to both Senator Trumbull and Congressman Washburne in mid-December.

Hon. L. Trumbull.

My dear Sir: Let there be no compromise on the question of extending slavery. If there be, all our labor is lost, and, ere long, must be done again. The dangerous ground—that into which some of our friends have a hankering to run—is Pop. Sov. Have none of it. Stand firm. The tug has to come, & better now, than any time hereafter. Yours as ever.

A. Lincoln

Hon. E. B. Washburne

My dear Sir. Your long letter received. Prevent, as far as possible, any of our friends from demoralizing themselves, and our cause, by entertaining propositions for compromise of any sort, on "slavery extension." There is no possible compromise upon it, but which puts us under again, and leaves all our work to do over again. Whether it be a Mo. line, or Eli Thayer's Pop. Sov. it is all the same. Let either be done, & immediately filibustering and extending slavery recommences. On that point hold firm, as with a chain of steel. Yours as ever.

A. Lincoln

In early February, the time came for Molly, me, and our boys to leave Springfield and journey by train to Washington for my inauguration set for March 4, 1861. We were in a time of uncertainty, and I believed we needed to be cautious. There were calls for me to speak about the crisis, but I preferred to wait.

There were two special people with whom I wished to spend a little time before I left.

The first was my step-mother, Sally, who still lived just south of Charleston in Coles County.

I took the train to Charleston and then a horse and buggy to her home, where she was living with Col. Augustus Chapman, her grandson by marriage. We spent a lovely afternoon talking about our years together in Indiana and in Illinois before I left for New Salem. We visited my father's grave and embraced warmly when it was time for me to leave.

The second was Billy Herndon.

We were standing on the stairs outside our office.

"Billy," I asked him, "how long have we been together?'"

"Over sixteen years," he replied.

"We've never had a cross word during all that time, have we?"

"No, indeed we have not."

I pointed to the signboard on the landing.

"Let it hang there undisturbed. Give our clients to understand that the election of a president makes no change in the firm of Lincoln and Herndon. If I live, I'm coming back here some time, and then we'll go right on practicing law as if nothing had ever happened."

The morning of February 11, 1861, was cold and rainy. Our friends gathered at the Great Western Railway station to wish us well as we boarded our train for Washington. The engine bell rang, I spoke a few words of farewell, and the train whistled and left for Washington.

On March 4, 1861, I was inaugurated as the 16th president of the United States.

As I stepped to the podium to deliver my inaugural address, I was lost for a moment. I was still wearing my top hat. This was a serious breach of protocol. I didn't know what to do. I started to fumble with it, and then, from the corner of my eye, I saw someone stepping up to hold it for me. I turned and realized it was Judge Douglas.

Epilogue

A True Friend of His Country and Its President

It was late March in 1861. I had been president for three weeks, and I had a visitor whom John Nicolay scheduled for the late afternoon. The weather was cold, windy, and raw—"pneumonia weather" a friend called it long ago in Illinois. I was sitting by the fireplace in my office, which was rapidly becoming my favorite spot in the White House.

John knocked on the door and escorted my guest to the chair adjacent to mine.

His face was haggard and pale, his posture slouched, and his gait slow and uncertain. As John seated him next to me, he grunted and wheezed.

"Judge Douglas," I said, "thank you for stopping by."

"Mr. President," he responded uncertainly, "thank you for inviting me."

"Judge, please dispense with 'Mr. President' and just call me 'Lincoln,' as in the old days."

"Thank you, Lincoln," he answered. "You don't happen to have a bottle of bourbon in the people's house, do you?"

"Indeed we do. How would you like it served?"

"Just in a glass, no fixings."

He took a gulp and began by saying, "Lincoln, I came here today as a Union man prepared to support you in any way I can. I will not vote for any Republican proposal or program. I am a Democrat. You know that, but you are a Union man too, and you deserve every bit of support you can get."

"Thank you, Judge," I said. "I am deeply appreciative. I will call on you when I need you, which will be quite often. I expect party men to be partisan. One of my tasks is to help build the Republican Party, and you, of all politicians, can understand that, but for you to cross the aisle and extend your support, particularly after the partisan battles we have waged against each other, is putting country ahead of party. That's an example for others on both sides to follow."

"Thank you, my good man."

He relaxed in the chair and followed my example of elevating his feet and legs on the fireplace fender. His boots were worn, and holes had begun to form on their soles.

"Ah, Lincoln," he sighed, "who would have thought that the two of us, both of whom came to the West to seek our fortunes, both of whom settled in Springfield, both of whom adored politics; who would have thought we would contend mightily for the sake of leading our country in its dark hour?"

"Yes, Judge, I've always thought that was most remarkable."

"And my good man, I have been asking why it is you sitting in the president's chair and not I."

"Judge, it may surprise you, but I've been asking myself the same question."

He gasped, wheezed, and coughed, and finally, when he cleared his throat several times, he could speak again.

"You know, if your party had run Seward, I would have won."

"I think that's quite possible. You would have won the swing states, which is why my party chose me. When Davis told me everything that happened at the convention, I couldn't believe I was nominated."

"It might have gone to the House, but I think I would have won outright."

"You may well be right."

"But that didn't happen, and it has fallen to you. I still don't understand it. As you said yourself, I was so far ahead of you in the race of ambition."

"Do you really want to know why I think it happened?"

"Of course."

"You were Macbeth and I was Hamlet."

"Lincoln, the Shakespearean!"

"You know your Shakespeare as well, Judge."

"I suppose what you are telling me is that I was too ambitious and you were more methodical—the wolf in sheep's clothing, as it were."

"For a long time I was beginning to think I was a sheep in sheep's clothing, but, as you know, I cast it off after the Kansas-Nebraska Act. There's nothing like a purpose, or even a mission where you can submerge your ambition. It gives you the drive and the energy, but it's not for ambition's sake."

"Yes, you may be right. My goal was to purge the country of slavery agitation, but unfortunately I made it worse."

"It is ironic, if you hadn't passed the Kansas-Nebraska Act, I would have remained a failed frontier politician. You might have been the most brilliant politician our country has produced. You were so young you would have been president at some point."

"I was so looking forward to a presidency of transcontinental railroads and westward expansion," he said. "I didn't think slavery would expand. I expected the issue to die."

"I think you misread the mood of the country."

"Yes, there's that. You were Hamlet biding your time . . . listening . . . listening. I always remember that about you. And somehow you became a formidable debater—the best I ever faced."

"Thank you, Judge."

"Lincoln, I fear for you in the Washington jungle. You were courageous to appoint your opponents to the cabinet. They will eye you each day thinking what it would be like if they'd won. They are snakes."

"Better to have them in the room than baiting snares and delusions for me without my knowledge. I am green, but I've learned so much in the past six years."

"Lincoln, one piece of advice—be careful of trusting Seward. He is livid that he was beaten by 'a little prairie lawyer.'"

"I appreciate the personal advice."

"Well, my good friend, Hamlet, you are about to experience the state in ruins. It will be your *King Lear*. You will be painfully alone, but if anyone can survive it, it is you."

"Hamlet is alone. He has no one to rely on but himself."

"And I have no one now who understands me as well as you."

"Oh, Judge, how idyllic it all seems now. We were young men coming of age in a new country. The promise was so bright. Our country was young and spoke to us of possibility.

"We were that group of Springfield politicians gathering together in the evenings at the fireplace in Speed's store.

Four of us served in the House, you and Baker became senators, and now one of us is president."

The Judge leaned back in his chair, wheezed and coughed again, but was able to say, "Oh, Lincoln, it sped by so quickly."

"Judge, how is your health?"

"It's not good. As you know I broke the tradition and campaigned for president across the country. I've never been so exhausted in my life. I can see the wisdom of your staying in Springfield and giving a few speeches atop the stairway of the Capitol building. Then came secession and using my congressional leadership to try to keep the country together. We had very little sleep for six weeks. Little good it did for anyone."

"No, Judge, you stood up for the Union, and thank you for giving those speeches in the South denouncing secession."

He bent down, covered his face with his hands, and coughed into them.

From this distressing sight came the words, muttered through his hands, "Oh, Lincoln, I am a broken man."

"Judge, don't say that, we have a country to lead—together—united as brothers—the Union to save."

He pulled himself together and hobbled out of his chair. I walked with him to the office door.

As he left, he barked at me, "Remember, Lincoln, I won't support ONE of your programs."

I detected a hint of a smile as we shook hands warmly, and I handed him off to John Nicolay.

"Godspeed, Mr. President," he called to me.

"And Godspeed to you, Judge."

On May 1, we learned Douglas was sick, with what seemed at first to be a bad cold. On May 10, he was more seriously ill and confined to his bed, but he rallied on May 19. For the next two weeks he alternated between periods of being in danger and then being free from it. Unfortunately in early June, his condition turned grave, and on the morning of June 3, shortly after sunrise, with Adele by his side, Stephen Douglas died.

I lost a friend, a rival, a bitter enemy, and finally, a true friend of his country and its president.

Acknowledgments

Publishing a book is a team effort.

To my publisher, Josh Stevens, the captain of the Reedy Press team, go my respect, admiration, and thanks. Josh was more involved with the creation of this book. I appreciate his guidance through the outlining and composition processes. He was both critic and cheerleader, and his unerring sense of what makes a good narrative has been a blessing for me.

This is the third book for which Kathleen Dragan at Reedy has been my editor. Working with her is a delight. You know you have a good editor when she reports she almost fell asleep reading part one. Needless to say, there was major revision. Kathleen is my partner; she is tough and supportive—what every writer needs. She says it is her job to show me what's on the page, and that is what she does.

My thanks go to Barbara Northcott and the Reedy production team. Production is also creating, and Barb is a master at it.

Julie Lally and Nancy Milton are Reedy's dynamite PR team. They booked me with Charlie Brennan on KMOX, where Charlie asked me to come as Abe himself. Abe was able to parry a question from a listener who wanted him to agree that Joe Biden was a worse president than James Buchanan.

My thanks go to my team of Lincoln scholars. Bob Bray and Doug Wilson were early supporters. There's nothing like tea at Books on the Square with James Cornelius and Mark Pohlad. James gave me his signed copy of Robert Johannsen's biography of Stephen Douglas.

Jon White invited me to be on a panel with him at the Lincoln Forum. Michael Burlingame read the entire manuscript and did not fall asleep. Michael is legendary for his kindness to adventurers in Lincoln Land. There is no one like him.

My friend Marc Feigen read the notorious part one, closely edited the text, and gave me insight into where he found Lincoln and where he didn't.

To so many readers—both young and old(er)—who have sent emails and told me in person how much they've enjoyed reading my books, I am forever grateful.

Thanks as well to all the teachers, particularly Ashley Jones, Jana Bayne, and Megan Eschbach, who have invited me into their classrooms—in person and via Zoom. Finding such engaged children gives me hope that Lincoln's story can make a difference in the 21st century.

It's also a treat to teach the books at Washington University's Osher Lifelong Learning program. My thanks to Janet Gillow, Denise Zona, and Tom Wack.

I give my thanks to my friends at the Lincoln Home National Historic Site from Tim Good, the site supervisor, to Amy Devaisher and Christy Blackwell in the site's store, to Ranger Isaiah and Mrs. Lincoln (Pam Brown). Amy is planning a book launch for Lincoln and Douglas at the annual birthday party for Mr. Lincoln in February. Loads of children attend! They'll probably buy *My Day with Abe Lincoln* by Jonathan White.

In the end it comes down to family and friends. My friends always ask how the book is coming, and my family puts up with me.

My deepest thanks go to my wife, Ginger. We've been together for forty years, and as a teacher, mom, friend to all, and spouse, she is the indispensable captain of my team.

Sources

This is a work of fiction.

I have, however, remained true to the historical record.

From the historical sources, I have chosen stories and insights that open a window into who Lincoln was as a person. I trust my intuitions, which have developed over the 14 years I've been working on this project. A good friend told me, "Abe is taking us on a journey." I'm humbled to be with him.

I find it remarkable that the two men who held the country's fate in their hands in the 1850s came from a postage stamp on the American map—Springfield, Illinois. Their story is one of intense political rivalry, but it also has a personal side—they knew each other well over their 25-year relationship.

The hardest part of this book was to remember that I was writing for young adults. I wanted them to know the history of the 1850s and the issues that tore the country apart, but I didn't want to overwhelm them. They can be challenged by a text that has an historical context and calls for familiarity with the Bible and Shakespeare, but my experience is that they do best when they are called on to think about and reflect on life. Lincoln's story appeals to them.

Michael Burlingame's epic *Abraham Lincoln: A Life* and Robert Johannsen's comprehensive *Stephen A. Douglas* were indispensable sources for this book. Basler's (ed.) *Collected Works of Lincoln* and Johannsen's (ed.) *Letters of Stephen A. Douglas* along with newspapers, diaries, journals, documents, and legal papers were my primary sources.

Above all, I am indebted to the scholars who are at work each day in the field of Lincoln studies. They are the heroes who make it possible for me to offer my "widow's mite" to our appreciation of our 16th president. The notes that follow are a tribute to their work. In most of the documents which Lincoln authored, I have kept his original spelling and punctuation.

Abbreviations and Short titles employed in notes:

Burlingame, *AL: A Life*: Michael Burlingame, *Abraham Lincoln: A Life, Volume One* (Baltimore: Johns Hopkins University Press, 2008).

CWL: Roy P. Basler, ed., *The Collected Works of Abraham Lincoln*, 9 vols., (New Brunswick, NJ: Rutgers University Press, 1953–55).

Preface

v "My friends— . . . " *CWL*, 4:190.

Part One

Chapter 1

5 We looked like so many fish . . . *CWL*, 1:260.

11 George "Old Buster" Robertson . . . Sidney Blumenthal, *Wrestling with His Angel: 1849–1856* (New York: Simon & Schuster, 2017), 33.

15 They fetch a hefty price. David Reynolds, *Abe: Abraham Lincoln in His Times* (New York: Penguin Press, 2020), 330–33.

Chapter 2

24 " . . . which lacked center and upper panels." Burlingame, *AL: A Life*, 310.

27 "At the end of the evening . . . " Paul Simon, *Lincoln's Preparation for Greatness* (Norman: University of Oklahoma Press, 1965), 55.

28 Upon first meeting him . . . George Fort Milton, *The Eve of Conflict* (New York and Boston: Houghton Mifflin, 1934), 2–3.

29 "a steam engine in britches." Milton, *The Eve of Conflict*, 25.

30 This is a new one, a slander case . . . *The Papers of Abraham Lincoln: Legal Documents and Cases*, ed. Daniel W. Stowell, Volume 2 (Charlottesville: University of Virginia Press, 2008), 161–163.

35 "I've got three walnuts . . . " Bonnie Paull & Richard Hart, *Lincoln's Springfield Neighborhood* (Charleston, SC: The History Press, 2015), 65.

35 Whose eyes brightened . . . Jon Meacham, *And There Was Light* (New York: Random House, 2022), 107.

37 . . . past the Dean, the Lyon, and the Beedle houses . . . Paull & Hart, *Lincoln's Springfield Neighborhood*, 5.

Chapter 3

40 "Eat, Molly, for we must live." Jean Baker, *Mary Todd Lincoln* (New York, W. W. Norton), 126.

40 I felt that if we should be the parents of twenty children . . . Burlingame, *AL: A Life*, 359.

44 She frowned at me, picked up her cup of coffee . . . Michael Burlingame, *An American Marriage* (New York; Pegasus, 2021), 51.

45 and the smash of a hard object, Ibid., 71.

45 I walked past the Carrigan home . . . Paull & Hart, *Lincoln's Springfield Neighborhood*, 5.

48 "This is God's curse on slavery!" Harriet Beecher Stowe, *Uncle Tom's Cabin* (New York: Barnes & Noble, 2021), 48.

51 I sincerely hope Father may yet recover his health; *CWL*, 2: 96–97.

52 "The huge green fragment of ice . . . Stowe, *Uncle Tom's Cabin*, 78.

52 " . . . If she's got a young un to be sold . . . Stowe, *Uncle Tom's Cabin*, 85.

Chapter 4

60 With my good friend, Grant Goodrich . . . Douglas L. Wilson and Rodney O. Davis, eds., *Herndon's Informants* (Urbana: University of Illinois Press, 1998), 509.

60 The trial lasted two weeks. *Legal Papers of Abraham Lincoln* (website), Parker vs. Hoyt, Document 129693.

61 "I will lie here until I rot . . . Wilson and Davis, eds. *Herndon Informants*, 510.

62 I believed the patent system . . . *CWL*, 3: 363.

63 "I hate him," said Legree . . . Stowe, *Uncle Tom's Cabin*, 488.

63 'Hark 'e, Tom . . . " Stowe, *Uncle Tom's Cabin*, 492.

64 In Stafford County, Virginia . . . pbs.org/wgbh/aia/part4/4p2915.html

66 . . . and we all knew him as Billy the Barber, Michael Burlingame, *The Black Man's President* (New York: Pegasus, 2021), 5–7.

67 WM. FLORVILLE, BARBER & HAIRDRESSER . . . Billy's advertisement appears on a Looking for Lincoln weather protected poster in Springfield, IL.

73 something called a madstone. Keith Sutton, "The interesting history of madstones," River Valley and Ozark, 2/15/2015: arkansasonline.com/news/2015/feb/15/interesting-history-madstones

74 a politician called Daniel Webster. Don E. and Virginia Fehrenbacher, *Recollected Words of Abraham Lincoln* (Stanford: Stanford University Press, 1996), 87.

Chapter 5

80 "It may be that the madstone cured him . . . Wilson and Davis, eds. *Herndon's Informants*, 182.

80 " . . . and you can meet my friend Mrs. Hillis. Douglas L. Wilson and Rodney O. Davis, eds. *Herndon's Lincoln* (Urbana: University of Illinois Press, 2006), 218.

85 'a criminal betrayal of precious rights . . . presidency.ucsb.edu/documents/appeal-the-independent-democrats-congress-the-people-the-united-states

87 I had read about it in the newspapers and in Uncle Tom's Cabin . . . I have based my idea that Lincoln was familiar with *Uncle Tom's Cabin* on the following pages from David Reynold's book *Abe: Abraham Lincoln in His Times*, 326, 335, and 365–367.

Part 2

Chapter 6

95 . . . from effigies of him that were burning. Ronald White, *A. Lincoln* (New York, Random House, 2009), 197.

95 We were thunderstruck and stunned. nps.gov/liho/learn/historyculture/peoriaspeech.htm

96 Jayne did go to the paper . . . Wilson and Davis, eds., *Herndon's Informants*, 266.

96 . . . so would help Yates. Michael Burlingame, *Abraham Lincoln: A Life*, ed. Jonathan W. White (Baltimore, Johns Hopkins University Press, 2023), 172.

97 I began to study Euclid's Elements, *Euclid's Elements*: Book 1, ed. Dana Densmore (Santa Fe: Green Cat Books, 2015), vii.

99 Douglas climbed through a first floor window . . . Lewis Lehrman, *Lincoln at Peoria* (Mechanicsburg, PA: Stackpole Press, 2008), 56.

100 I called to them to go home . . . Ibid., 55.

100 I wish to say that I do not propose to question the patriotism . . . all excerpts from Lincoln's Peoria Speech come from *CWL* 2: 247–283.

Chapter 7

110 . . . and his heart knew no boundary. Willard, L. King, *Lincoln's Manager David Davis* (Cambridge, MA: Harvard University Press, 1960), xi.

110 . . . having the last word as usual. *AL: A Life*, 331.

111 . . . became a school teacher and practiced law. Willard King, *Lincoln's Manager David Davis*, 67.

111 "It was the profoundest speech . . . " *AL: A Life*, 387.

112 " . . . a speaker acquit himself . . . " *AL: A Life*, 389.

114 "When it comes to this . . . " *CWL* 2: 323.

117 "No, but I am temperate . . . " *AL: A Life*, 377.

Chapter 8

125 That fall, I joined . . . Wilson and Davis, eds., *Herndon's Informants*, 732.

127 "I'd estimate . . . " *AL: A Life*: 397.

132 "Smith also hasn't forgiven Lincoln . . . " *AL: A Life*, 397.

132 "Shields said it was . . . " David Donald, *Lincoln* (New York, Simon and Schuster, 1995), 180.

132 " . . . Charles Henry Ray aboard." *AL: A Life*, 395.

135 "Hold steady . . . " *AL: A Life*, 401.

137 He couldn't forgive Judd and Palmer . . . *AL: A Life*, 402.

139 A less good humored man . . . *CWL* 2: 307.

139 It wasn't in my nature . . . *AL: A Life*, 403.

139 "Not too disappointed . . . " *AL: A Life*, 403.

Chapter 9

146 He alleged patent infringement . . . *Lincoln Lore*, Number 1516, Ft. Wayne, IN, June 1964.

146 . . . Edwin Stanton to be . . . *AL: A Life*, 339.

147 . . . examining Manny's machine . . . *CWL* 2: 315.

148 "Let that fellow go with his gang." *AL: A Life*, 340.

148 "Why is that long-armed baboon . . . " *AL: A Life*, 340.
149 "Come on then . . . " David Potter, *The Impending Crisis* (New York: Harper, 1976), 199.
149 "to kill every . . . " Ibid., 203.
150 "Beecher's Bibles . . . " Ibid., 206–207.
150 "You enquire . . . " *CWL* 2: 322–323.
152 The runaway slave . . . poets.org/poem/song-myself-10
153 "Kansas is in flames . . . " Ronald White, *A. Lincoln*, 218.
154 Sherriff Jones and his posse . . . *New York Tribune*, May 30, 1856, 4.
155 By the news from Washington . . . loc.gov/resource/sn83030213/1856-05-23/ed-1/?sp=4&r=0.117,0.402,0.708,0.25,0
156 . . . disapproving of nativist prejudice. Michael Burlingame, *AL: A Life*, 191.
157 . . . to end slavery gradually . . . Ibid., 142.
160 Walter L. Dayton of New Jersey . . . Ibid., 194.

Chapter 10

162 We were just about to turn right . . . Jesse W. Weik, *The Real Lincoln* (Lincoln: University of Nebraska Press, 2002), 101.
162 "William Wallace Lincoln . . . " Paull & Hart, *Lincoln's Springfield Neighborhood*, 65.
165 I was also right that he would try to weasel . . . Benjamin P. Thomas, *Abraham Lincoln* (New York, Barnes & Noble, 1994), 174.
165 "Now I protest . . . *CWL* 2: 405.
166 "We will be ready . . . Burlingame, *Abraham Lincoln: A Life*, 156.
167 Douglas has broken with Buchanan . . . Ibid., 204.
167 "his course has not been merely right— . . . Ibid., 205.
168 "Billy, we must never sell old friends . . . Ibid., 206.
168 "We want to govern ourselves in our own way . . . Ibid., 205
168 "Douglas's abuse of us . . . Ibid., 205.
168 "Give Mr. Lincoln my regards when you return and tell him I have . . . Ibid., 206.
169 "Douglas has abused and betrayed the North . . . Ibid., 207.
169 "He is the greatest liar . . . " Ibid., 207.
171 "A house divided against itself . . . *CWL* 2: 461-462.

Chapter 11

177 "If you desire negro citizenship . . . Douglas Wilson and Rodney O. Davis, eds., *The Lincoln-Douglas Debates* (Urbana: University of Illinois Press, 2008), 14.
177 "Why can it not exist divided . . . Ibid.,13.
178 "by lawful means . . . Ibid., 58.
179 "He tries to weasel his way . . . Ibid., 58.
180 appearance of Donati's comet . . . Ibid., 84.
181 I say, that Judge Douglas and his friends . . . Ibid., 100.
181 I will say then that I am not . . . Ibid., 131.
182 'Exhausted to the dregs . . . hd.housedivided.dickinson.edu/node/16668
188 I hold that the signers . . . Wilson and Davis, eds., *The Lincoln-Douglas Debates*, 266.

188 The real issue . . . Ibid., 282.
188 That is the real issue . . . Ibid., 284.
189 I care more for the great principle of self-government . . . Ibid., 291.
190 I am glad I made the late race . . . *CWL* 3: 339

Part 3
Chapter 12
196 " . . . a rustic on his way to the circus. Willard King, *David Davis Lincoln's Manager*, 27.
197 "Our friend Lincoln has recently made a noble canvass . . . John M. Hay and John G. Nicolay, *Abraham Lincoln, A History*, Vol. II (New York: Cosimo, 2009) 177.
197 Just think of such a Sucker as me as president. In the 19th century, Sucker = inhabitant of Illinois as Hoosier = inhabitant of Indiana.
198 'There are two giants in Illinois . . . ' Ronald White, *A. Lincoln*, 292.
198 " . . . but there is no such good luck in store for me . . . ", Ibid., 293.
199 " . . . it is a proposition in proportion . . . *CWL* 3: 432.
201 " . . . on a cruise ship underneath him." David Reynolds, *Abe: Abraham Lincoln in His Times*, 458.
202 'STEP TO THE RIGHT,' Ibid., 458.

Chapter 13
For this chapter I have relied on Michael Burlingame, *AL: A Life*, pages 342–346, particularly the dialogue on pages 344–345, and John Evangelist Walsh, *Moonlight* (New York: St. Martin's Press, 2000).

Chapter 14
222 "We desire to head off the little gentleman." Ronald White, *A. Lincoln*, 299.
223 "He is so put up by nature . . . " *AL: A Life*, 565–566.
224 "A most extraordinary telegraphic bulletin . . . " *New York Daily Tribune*, October 18, 1859, page 4.
224 Over the next few days . . . nps.gov/articles/john-browns-raid.htm
228 Hon. A. Lincoln, Harold Holzer, *Lincoln at Cooper Union* (New York: Simon & Schuster, 2005), 10.
229 It would take a miracle . . . Title of Edward Achorn, *The Lincoln Miracle* (New York: Atlantic Monthly Press, 2023).
230 "That alone is impetus enough for me . . . " Holzer, *Lincoln at Cooper Union*, xix–xx.

Chapter 15
240 The Debates in the Several States Conventions . . . James Kent's Commentaries . . . Holzer, *Lincoln at Cooper Union*, 51–52.
242 On the morning of February 22 . . . Ibid., 58–65.

Chapter 16
247 The afternoon and early evening in New York . . . Ibid., 103.
247 . . . my new clothes hung on me . . . Don and Virginia Fehrenbacher, *Recollected Words of Abraham Lincoln*, 253.
247 "The facts with which I shall deal this evening . . . " All quotations from the Cooper Union Address come from *CWL* 3: 522–550.

252 "That was the best political speech . . . *AL: A Life*, 587.
255 "I am informed . . . Ibid., 598.
256 a small part of the roof . . . Thomas, *Abraham Lincoln*, 207
256 . . . but I can say that I've mauled . . . *AL: A Life*, 598.
257 " . . . that Abraham Lincoln is the first choice . . . " Ibid., 599.

Chapter 17
267 "Illinois Headquarters" Achorn, *The Lincoln Miracle*, 14.
268 Things are working; keep a good nerve— . . . loc.gov/resource/mal.0265700/?st=pdf&r=-0.21,-0.078,1.42,1.42,0
268 I take great satisfaction in assuring you . . . loc.gov/resource/mal.0266200/?st=pdf&r=-0.327,-0.31,1.654,1.654,0
269 . . . I was not as rusty as I thought. Edward Achorn, *The Lincoln Miracle*, 296–297.
270 Things are working admirably well now. loc.gov/resource/mal.0265300/?st=text&r=-0.55,-0.091,2.101,1.418,0
271 The are quiet but moving heaven & Earth . . . loc.gov/resource/mal.0266800/?st=text
273 Am very hopeful . . . picryl.com/media/david-davis-to-abraham-lincoln-thursday-may-17-1860-telegram-concerning-chicago
274 Special to the *Illinois State Journal* idnc.library.illinois.edu/?a=d&d=SJO18600518.1.2&e=-------en-20--1--txt-txIN----------
275 "I don't like the looks of it . . ." *AL: A Life*, 622.
276 "I think the convention will nominate me . . . " Ibid., 623
276 Your nominated . . . loc.gov/resource/mal.0272100/?r=-0.61,-0.024,2.221,0.749,0
277 "There's a little woman down at our house . . . " Edward Achorn, *The Lincoln Miracle*, 352.

Chapter 18
280 Bell's support would probably come . . . Ronald White, *A. Lincoln*, 333.
284 I was able to hire John Nicolay . . . Ibid., 337.
285 . . . to carry New York for Douglas . . . *CWL* 4: 98.
285 I had not heard a word from Rhode Island for a long time . . . *CWL* 4:97.
286 Mr. Dubois has shown me your letter . . . *CWL* 4: 132–133.
287 My father has just home from the fair . . . *CWL* 4:130.
288 Your very agreeable letter . . . *CWL* 4: 129.

Chapter 19
296 Let there be no compromise on the question of extending slavery. *CWL* 4: 149.
297 My dear Sir. Your long letter received. *CWL* 4: 151.
297 . . . living with Col. Augustus Chapman . . . Wilson and Davis, eds., *Herndon's Informants*, 109.
298 "Let it hang there undisturbed . . . " *AL: A Life*, 757.